FRED'S FIVE MINUTE TALKS.

Your Masonic Questions Answered

Fred L

GW00569348

Lewis Masonic

First published 2013

ISBN 978 0 85318 437 9

All rights reserved. No part of this book may be reproduced or transmitted in any form or by any means, electronic or mechanical, including photocopying, recording, scanning or by any information storage and retrieval system, on the internet or elsewhere, without permission from the Publisher in writing.

© Fred Lomax 2013

Published by Lewis Masonic

an imprint of Ian Allan Publishing Ltd, Hersham, Surrey KT12 4RG.
Printed in England.
Visit the Lewis Masonic website at www.lewismasonic.co.uk

Distributed in the United States of America and Canada by BookMasters Distribution Services.

Copyright
Illegal copying and selling of publications deprives authors, publishers and booksellers of income, without which there would be no investment in new publications. Unauthorised versions of publications are also likely to be inferior in quality and contain incorrect information. You can help by reporting copyright infringements and acts of piracy to the Publisher or the UK Copyright Service.

Picture Credits
All pictures reproduced in the book are from the author's collection unless otherwise credited.

Dedication

By writing this book I have fulfilled a lifelong ambition and I dedicate it to the one who brings me joy every day, my wife Sheila, and to the other members of our families who have supported and encouraged me.

Contents

Lord Lindsay

The frontispiece of this book shows a photograph of a collar jewel worn by the Master of Lindsay Lodge No. 1335 in the Province of West Lancashire, so named 'The Lindsay Jewel' in honour of the man whom the Lodge was named after.

James Ludovic Lindsay was born on 28 July 1847 at Saint-Germain-en-Laye, Île-de-France, and was the son of Alexander William Crawford Lindsay, 25th Earl of Crawford and Margaret Lindsay. He was baptised in the local Episcopalian Church.

In due course he married Emily Florence Bootle-Wilbraham, daughter of Col. Hon. Edward Bootle-Wilbraham and Emily Ramsbottom at St. George's Church, Hanover Square, London on 22 July 1869 and with whom he had seven children. He lived in the family home at Haigh Hall, Wigan, Lancashire, and at a house in London.

His education was at Eton College and Trinity College, Cambridge University. He served as a Lieutenant in the Grenadier Guards and was a Member of Parliament for Wigan between 1874 and 1880. He was made a Fellow of the

Lord Lindsay – a caricature from
Vanity Fair, 1878

Royal Society in 1878 and appointed President of the Royal Astronomical Society 1878-1880, and he succeeded to the title of 9th Earl of Balcarres and 26th Earl of Crawford in the same year. In addition he succeeded to the title Lord Lindsay and Balneil and 3rd Baron of Wigan of Haigh Hall, County of Lancaster. In 1891 he was made a Knight of the Order of the Thistle (KT).

He joined the Lodge of Antiquity, No. 178 at Wigan on 3 January 1867 and as Lord Lindsay he was the first Worshipful Master and Founder of Lindsay Lodge No. 1335, named after him, in 1870.

The jewel was presented to the Lodge in 1873, having been specially commissioned and manufactured in Birmingham of solid silver. It bears his coat of arms with the motto *Astra Castra Numen Lumen*, translated as *The Stars are my camp, the Deity my light*. It was always worn attached to the Master's collar until Lindsay Lodge merged with Bryn Lodge No. 6553 in 2009.

He was the Centenary Worshipful Master of the Lodge of Antiquity No. 178 in 1886 and he rose to Masonic eminence to become Deputy Provincial Grand Master of the Province of West Lancashire in 1888.

He died in London on 31 January 1913 and Crawford Lodge No. 3728, sadly now closed, was named in his memory.

Haigh Hall (pronounced 'Hay') was for many years the English seat and ancestral home of the Lindsay family, the Earls of Crawford & Balcarres. The present hall, built between 1827 and 1840, currently has an 'English Heritage Register' designation. Haigh Hall and its grounds were bought by Wigan Council in 1947 and now make up one of the region's most beautiful country parks.

Acknowledgements

The topics in this book are very varied and during my research I have called upon the works of many eminent Masonic scholars including:

Neville Barker Cryer, Harry Carr, Bernard Jones, Frederick Smyth, Roy Wells, Harry Mendoza, J. S. M. Ward, Richard Sandbach, S. Brent Morris, Robert Macoy, Prof. Andrew Prescott, Wallace McLeod, Colin Dyer, Julian Rees and others. To all those who have gone down the path of Masonic research before me and have provided me with an endless source of material, I am extremely grateful.

To John Acaster for kindly agreeing to write the foreword to this book and for his support for the idea initially.

To my good friend and fellow author Dr. David Harrison for his help and guidance and to another good friend Derek Hunt for his excellent photographs. To Kai Hughes for the opportunity to photograph other fraternities' regalia. To Charles Vaughan, Grand Master of the Odd Fellows, Manchester Unity for allowing me to photograph their regalia and jewels.

To the Masonic Order of Athelstan for the 'lost' symbols of Craft Masonry.

To my many friends and colleagues in the Provinces of West and East Lancashire, who have encouraged and supported me throughout this project, and to the two Provinces themselves for giving me permission to use the pageantry photographs from their websites.

Finally, to my son Andrew, who made my life much easier by proof reading each of the stories in the book and helping me put together the final draft.

About the author – Frederick Charles Lomax

The author was initiated into a Lodge at Westhoughton near Bolton, in the Province of West Lancashire, in the mid-1970s. He later joined a Lodge in Wigan, his home town, becoming its Master in 1999. Later he became Secretary of the Lodge until its amalgamation in 2007.

He also joined Blackburn Lodge in the adjoining Province of East Lancashire and became its Master in 2003 and Secretary a year later until it closed in 2007. In the meantime he was accepted as a member of the Manchester Lodge for Masonic Research and he was its Master in 2009 and the President of the Manchester Association for Masonic Research in the same year.

Quite uniquely he holds the rank of Past Provincial Junior Grand Warden in both Provinces, receiving them both within a month in 2011.

In East Lancashire he is the Provincial Grand Orator and serves on the main Education & Development committee as well as being Chairman of the Materials sub-committee which provides interesting papers on a wide variety of Masonic subjects including maintaining an up-to-date and comprehensive database of Masonic speakers. He is also the Chairman of the judges for the East Lancashire annual Short Papers Competition.

The Northern Conference has been held annually since 2008 in East Lancashire and increases in popularity every year. Fred is one of the original team of organisers.

In West Lancashire he is a Regional Publicity Officer looking after a team of six Group Publicity officers as well as using his extensive training experience to act as trainer to the Provincial Publicity team. In 2009 he was appointed as the Provincial Coordinator of the United Grand Lodge initiative, the Historical Records Survey, achieving a returns percentage of 82% from the largest province in the country. He also maintains an up-to-date database of speakers similar to his role in his sister province.

In 2008 he organised a successful four month long exhibition 'Freemasonry – It's No Secret' in conjunction with the Wigan & Leigh Leisure and Culture Trust in the town's Heritage Museum which attracted many non-Masonic visitors.

He has written numerous papers on Masonic subjects and is a regular speaker throughout the north of England. He has written several articles for The Square Masonic magazine and his 'Five Minute Papers' appear as a regular quarterly feature.

In the Mark degree he is a Past Provincial Officer and a member of the Royal Arch. In the Masonic Order of Athelstan he is a Past Grand Sword Bearer.

Before retiring Fred was a Business Consultant specialising in the Care sector and when he is not involved in Masonic activities he enjoys golf, photography and walking.

Foreword

This is a book which is much needed. When I first joined Freemasonry I was very puzzled by many things which other members of my Lodge seemed to find quite normal. I was only too aware of my ignorance. It made me feel uneasy for a long time. What had I let myself in for? While the atmosphere was friendly and there was much to admire, why were people using terms and doing things apparently so naturally that were nevertheless odd and difficult to understand? What did it all mean? I could quite easily have left.

Fred's Five Minute Talks should help to allay this queasy feeling of inadequacy. It is like a multipack of crisps. Fred has prepared a series of convenient crunchy bites suited to the hectic life-style of our times. His writing is quite straightforward, to the point, and easy to understand. The information he gives is trustworthy and relevant. Every paper is stamped with his friendly, questing, proudly-Lancashire personality. There is flavour in these crisps.

The book is timely. It is a god-send to the Mentor. The recent initiative by the United Grand Lodge of England to spread Masonic knowledge by the general use of mentors should be greatly helped by the appearance of this book. Here is a ready source of inspiration and reference, and a handy means of instituting a regular programme of varied snippets into the ordinary course of Lodge activity. Indeed, if circumstances allow, each paper could form a basis for discussion, with added comment and knowledge supplied from the experience of those within the room.

My hope is that brethren will be stimulated into developing an appetite for Masonic knowledge, will generally want more; that some will be particularly stimulated to find more, that our Masonic libraries will actually be used; that a few will follow up some aspect and that in consequence more such 'Five Minute Papers', perhaps with a slant from Bristol, or from Newcastle, or from Canterbury, will be added to our store of enjoyment. Some may be drawn into becoming members of Research associations, such as the Manchester Association of which Fred has been President. A number may like to write more fully. There is plenty of help available to assist that process, such as the series of one-day courses being mounted by Quatuor Coronati Lodge in London from November 2012 onwards.

The reality, brethren, is that Freemasonry is rich in excitement for those that want to discover. It is an ocean which few do more than dip their toes in and splash about. But the wonders of the deep are astonishing to those who merely snorkel. The breadth of the subject stretches round the world. Few countries have been untouched by the wave that London set in motion 300 years ago.

I didn't leave. I learnt. Gradually I became knowledgeable. Slowly I began to value the oddity which I had joined. Imperceptibly it broadened my humanity and extended my spirituality. I have voyaged. I would gladly wish the same for others. I hope that *Fred's Five Minute Talks* will provide the helping hand, the *Ahimon Rezon*, for those who need it and a compass by which to illuminate their course.

John Acaster
Chairman, Q.C. Correspondence Circle Ltd.;
Member of Quatuor Coronati Lodge No. 2076;
Past President of the Manchester Association for Masonic Research

Introduction

My intention in compiling the papers for this book was to encourage the enquiring Mason to gain a better understanding of the Craft in an easy and readable form. There are many things which confuse a new member of the Craft and we have a duty to provide as much information as possible to enhance their early experiences. There will also be those who have been in Freemasonry for some years who will benefit from the information made available to them.

As each topic in this book is free standing it is an ideal companion for the Lodge Mentor, which will enable him to answer the many and varied questions likely to be asked by the new or less experienced Mason.

Mentoring has been established across most Lodges in England and Wales and has been given high priority by the United Grand Lodge of England in its initiative on recruitment and the retention of existing members. This book fully supports that initiative.

It is also designed to enable a Lodge, should it wish, to have any of them delivered in open Lodge without taking up too much time in the proceedings.

CHAPTER 1

A Fit and Proper Person to be Made a Mason

We hear that phrase used regularly in our Lodges but what does it mean?

The Old Charges stipulated that to be a mason you had to be of 'honest parentage' or 'of good kindred' - in other words not illegitimate. We must not forget that in this context we are talking about the medieval mason working on a church, abbey or some other great building in which the church would be involved and to be of 'doubtful' birth was unacceptable in those days. But what else would bar a man from being a fit and proper person? Well the obvious one is not having a belief in a Supreme Being. If there is any doubt at all in the minds of those interviewing a potential candidate they should err on the side of caution and not accept him.

But what of character? Is he a fit and proper person? Do we look closely enough into the character of a man applying to join the Craft? I fear not is sometimes the answer. W. L. Wilmshurst, in his book *The Meaning of Masonry*, said: '*…it is obvious that special qualifications of mind and intention are essential in a candidate of the type likely to be benefited by the Order in the way that its doctrine contemplates…*'

Today, we ask the potential candidate to sign a declaration on Application Form P to say that he has not, amongst other things, been the subject of criminal or similar proceedings. If he cannot make such a declaration, a statement must be sent to the Grand Secretary for a certificate to be issued that the circumstances are such that it would not constitute a bar to Initiation. Obviously, if there are any doubts at all the application should not be allowed to go ahead.

What about a 'fit and proper person' in the physical sense? At one time, a person who was not whole of limb could not be accepted either as a working mason or as a speculative Freemason.

Until relatively recently in the USA, this was still a requirement in Craft Lodges and was strictly applied. Many a good man, because of a physical disability, although quite acceptable in every other sense, could be turned away. It is regrettable that these Lodges took this view, albeit a misguided one in our eyes, but they adhered to the medieval interpretation of a 'fit and proper person'.

Thankfully, we no longer discriminate in this manner and there are many men who a few years ago would have been refused admission to our Order that have joined the Craft and given valuable service without detriment to themselves or their connections. Obviously every case must be judged on its merits and the test must be: would the candidate be 'incapable of learning the art'?

Finally, the late great Harry Carr recalled the story of a bright young candidate who was asked: *'Do you believe in God?'* He replied, after some hesitation: *'Well, it depends on what you mean by God.'* The committee appeared to be shocked by what seemed to be a rather careless or casual reply. However, the WM remained unruffled, and quietly continued:

'No. Mr........ it depends on what YOU mean by God.'

The candidate was a good talker, but he talked himself out of that Lodge and was not admitted.

Absent Brethren

The toast to Absent Brethren is often given at a festive board at a fixed time and is commonly known in some Lodges as 'The Nine O'clock Toast'. However, regrettably, the timing of the toast is not always as it should be and invariably it has to fit in with the proceedings of the evening. As the hands of the clock at 9 o'clock represent an angle of 90°, it is another of those Masonic associations which we Masons like to make. However, I have known Brethren, who, when they have been away from home, have drunk a toast at 9 o'clock in the evening to remember their colleagues at home and I have done the same myself.

Edward Still from Sussex advised me that its antiquity is not really known; however, he directed me to a reference in the minutes of the Lodge of Antiquity No 2 of 1759 in which it was recorded: '....the health of our absent members was drunk'. However, a 9 o'clock toast is not specifically mentioned. I understand that it was generally accepted that the toast 'Absent Brethren' actually came into prominence in England and Wales during the First World War, when so many of our Brethren were killed or injured in that terrible conflict.

In certain Provinces, the toast to Absent Brethren is accompanied by the singing of the hymn 'Eternal Father Strong to Save'. Only two verses of the hymn are sung, the first as here:

'Eternal Father, strong to save,
Whose arm hath bound the restless wave,
Who bidd'st the mighty ocean deep
Its own appointed limits keep;
Oh, hear us when we cry to Thee,
For those in peril on the sea.'

The toast is then given standing and 'To Absent Brethren'. In Liverpool and adjacent areas it is given as 'To Absent and Seafaring Brethren'. In the north of Lancashire the toast is given at 10 o'clock, as many Lodges do not tile until 7.00pm making it impractical to have a toast at nine. This is also given to 'Absent and Seafaring Brethren'.

I am also advised that in Hampshire, at least one Lodge used to sing two verses of 'Architect, In Thy Great Mercy, Hear Our Anxious Prayer' and in one East Midlands Province there is a Lodge which does toast 'Absent Brethren' - but seated and in silence.

Another variant of the toast I have come across, which is sung in a London Lodge, is:

'Brethren, shall we pause a while and be of one accord,
To note those who are missing from this our Festive Board?
Shall we think of absent brethren and take a draught of wine,
And hope that they do likewise, at the very stroke of nine?'

There are several variations and even poems related to the toast which unfortunately are too long for a short paper such as this.

Sadly, however, the use of the toast to Absent Brethren is not universal in England and Wales, which is unfortunate.

Almoner and Charity Steward

The Almoner

The Almoner remains an active and important office in Masonic Lodges in England. His duty is to oversee the needs of the Brethren within his Lodge. He is the contact for Charity and looks after the welfare of the members, including carrying out visits to the sick, aged and infirm.

The term 'Almoner' is derived from the Old French word *aumônier*. In England, church almoners were responsible for distributing alms to the poor. Bishops had their own almoners. Almoners were also attached to the courts of the Kings of France. Charles VIII even had a Grand Almoner.

Today, the Anglican Lord High Almoner is the Bishop of Manchester, the Rt. Rev. Nigel McCulloch, who is responsible for organising the Queen's annual distribution of Maundy money on Maundy Thursday.

In Masonic terms, he is one of the additional officers in a Lodge. This office is one of the most important roles for a Mason to undertake. In certain Lodges with a large number of members or widows, there may be an Almoner and Assistant Almoners to cope with the workload. The latter is not yet an official appointment but they still have a vital part to play in looking after the welfare of members and widows.

The office of Almoner requires a great deal of qualities such as kindness, patience and discretion, as he is often dealing with very sensitive matters which may be financial, medical or emotional. He will be expected to report to the Lodge on a regular basis on matters concerning members and widows.

The Charity Steward

Charity Stewards only began to appear in Lodges around 1975, so it is a relatively new office. Like the Almoner, it is one of the additional offices in a Lodge, but nevertheless a very important one.

All Lodges have a duty to raise money for charity and it is the Charity Steward's responsibility to keep the Lodge informed of any charity events which may be taking place and encourage the Brethren to contribute. He will discuss with other members of the Lodge which particular causes should Lodge charity contributions be directed to and he will also make recommendations for the distribution of Masonic and non-Masonic donations.

It is the Charity Steward's responsibility to manage the administration, records and contacts and to be familiar with Constitutional requirements and Lodge byelaws with respect to Charity fund accounts kept by the Lodge and to maintain accurate records of all receipts and contributions made by members.

The Charity Steward must also ensure that contributions comply with Gift Aid regulations, when appropriate, and that completed documents are passed to the Province or District without delay. The Charity Steward is also responsible for liaising with the Lodge bank and tax office when needed.

Most Provinces have a Provincial Grand Almoner and Provincial Grand Charity Steward, in some cases supported by Regional and Group Charity Stewards in certain larger Provinces.

Ancient Charges and Regulations, Ancient Charges and the Old Charges

The first two can be found in the *Book of Constitutions* of the United Grand Lodge of England. But what are they? Where did they come from? How old are they? Are they really Ancient?

An Ancient Charge may be read in a Lodge, often after the minutes, as a reminder to Brethren to follow the Charges of a Freemason, but how many of us bother to actually read them? They can be found from page 147 in the *B of C*. However, they are different to the Ancient Charges and Regulations starting on page vii. These are the Ancient Charges and Regulations read to and acknowledged by the Master Elect at his Installation ceremony and are much shorter than the former. These are regulatory in nature, to which the Master Elect must acknowledge his consent before he can be installed into the Chair of King Solomon.

> *'An Ancient Charge, on the other hand, concerns a Freemason's moral duties,*
> *of God and Religion, of the Civil Magistrate,*
> *Supreme and Subordinate, of Lodges,*
> *of Masters, Wardens, Fellows and Apprentices,*
> *of behaviour: In the Lodge whilst constituted;*
> *After the Lodge is over and the Brethren not gone,*
> *When Brethren meet without, Strangers, but not in a Lodge;*
> *In the presence of Strangers, but not in a Lodge;*
> *At Home and in the Neighbourhood;*
> *And towards a strange Brother.'*

Those are the Ancient Charges used by many Lodges and it is likely that they were devised by the Rev. James Anderson when he wrote the first *Book of Constitutions* in 1723. However, he must have had some original material to have arrived at this moral code. George Payne, the second Grand Master in 1718, asked for any old documents pertaining to Craft to be brought in to show the usages in Ancient times - and this is where the Old Charges come in.

In fact, these are more ancient than the Ancient Charges. Numerous originals are still in existence, ranging from the *Regius MS* of 1390 and the *Cooke MS* of 1410 to *The Grand Lodge MS* of 1583, about 130 in all. Several were written in the seventeenth and eighteenth centuries, after the formation of the first Grand Lodge. Most have three sections, a prayer, a historical part and the charges. A famous one is the *Beswick-Royd MS* which was discovered in 1915 (now in the Museum at Freemasons Hall, Bridge Street, Manchester), which is believed to have been written in the early part of the 16th century on four strips of parchment, approximately six inches wide, stitched together to form a continuous strip 6ft 10in (2008mm) in length.

Historians believe that they are essentially English in origin and no other Craft than masonry possessed or used them.

Why don't you take a look at them next time you pick up your *Book of Constitutions*?

Bible Openings in the Lodge

According to the late Harry Carr in his book *The Freemason at Work* there is some variation in different parts of the country with regard to which pages the Bible should be opened at in a Lodge.

The first ever record in this country dates from the English exposure *Three Distinct Knocks* of 1760 for the three degrees, as follows:

1st Degree: the Second Epistle of Peter (with reference to brotherly kindness and charity)
2nd Degree: The story from Judges, chapter xii, of the test of the Ephraimites
3rd Degree: I Kings, chapter vii, the final details of Solomon's Pillars

In the 1920s Dr. Cartwright reported that in old Yorkshire Lodges it was customary to open the Bible at:

1st Degree: Psalm 133: 'Behold how good it is for brethren to dwell together in unity'
2nd Degree: Amos chapter vii v. 7: '…the Lord stood upon a wall made by plumb-line, with plumb-line in his hand'
3rd Degree: Ecclesiastes, chapter xii: 'Then the dust shall return to the earth as it was; and the spirit shall return unto God who gave it.

In Bristol - where the workings are very old - the following:

1st Degree: Ruth chapter ii, v. 119: The story of Ruth and Boaz
2nd Degree: Judges chapter xii, vv. 5,6: The test of the Ephraimites
3rd Degree: Genesis chapter iv, v. 22: The birth of Jabal and Jabul, who are mentioned in the Old Charges from c. 1400 onwards.

In Germany, many Lodges use:

1st Degree: John chapter I, v. 1: 'In the beginning was the word…'
2nd Degree: Matthew chapter xxii, v. 39: 'Thou shalt love thy neighbour as thyself.'
3rd Degree: II Chronicles chapter vi: Solomon's dedication of the Temple

Also in many old English workings it was common for the Bible to be opened at John I, 1, especially when seven degrees were worked: those of 1st, 2nd and 3rd, Mark, Excellent Master (Veils) Royal Arch and Knights Templar. It is important to remember that in many very old Lodges there were two Installations a year, when the Master only served six months: on St John the Baptist day 24 June and St John the Evangelist on 27 December; hence the name used by some Lodges for Installations as the 'Festival of St John.'

There is no official Grand Lodge ruling and few of the named rituals such as *The Perfect Ceremonies* actually specify which openings should be used, where the opening for all degrees is II Chronicles chapter vi as a standard opening which is also prescribed in the *English Ritual*. That particular passage deals with the preliminaries to the building of the Temple and of Solomon's first request to Hiram, King of Tyre for timber, etc. and a 'man cunning to work in gold, and in silver and in brass' etc.

Take a look at which openings your VSL has the page markers in, next time you go into your Lodge.

Calling Off and Calling On

Where does it come from? Well, we have to rely on the Masonic exposure of the early 1700s 'Three Distinct Knocks', which provides the earliest information about it. This is what it says:

> 'The Master whispers to the Senior Deacon at his right-hand side, and says: ' 'tis my will and pleasure that this Lodge is called off from work to refreshment during pleasure'; then the Deacon carries it to the Senior Warden and whispers the same words in his ear; he then whispers it in the ear of the Junior Deacon, and he carries it to the Junior Warden and whispers the same to him, who declares it with a loud voice and says: 'it is our Master's Will and Pleasure, that this Lodge is called from work to refreshment during pleasure'. Then he sets up his column and the Senior lays his down, for the care of the Lodge is in the hands of the Junior Warden while they are at refreshment.'

Raising and lowering of columns

There is a practical reason why the columns are used in this way. During the early years of speculative Masonry, Lodge work was done at a table and the

Tyler would serve drinks to the members during the time the Lodge was open. Toasts would be taken during a pause in the business; however, for a meal, which might be taken at the same table, the Lodge would be 'Called Off'.

If the Lodge was Called Off, the Brethren remained in their seats. A signal, recognisable by the Tyler to show that the Lodge had been Called Off would be necessary. How should this be done? By the use of the Wardens' Columns of course, and as we know they are raised and lowered at the Opening and Closing of the Lodge and the same applies when Calling Off and Calling On.

These days, of course, the whole thing is spoken out loud by the Master and Junior Warden and the single knock associated with it is done in *reverse*, i.e. the Junior Warden first then the Senior Warden and finally the Master as the Lodge is Called Off.

A Lodge may be 'Called Off' at the Master's discretion; it is not to be done in the middle of a ceremony and there is no particular degree associated with 'Calling Off'. The Board of General Purposes ruled on 8 March 1961 that: '...it recommends that the Master of a Lodge should be permitted to make a short break in the proceedings at a suitable time during a meeting provided that the Lodge is properly Called Off and Called On again.'

It is not uncommon in some old Lodges - who are inclined to start their Installation meeting early - for there to be a break at sometime during the Installation Ceremony, usually after the Inner Workings when Brethren take a comfort break. In the United States it is common for Lodges to Call Off for a 'libation'.

Finally, there is also a very practical purpose for 'Calling Off and On'. In some countries such as India and Australia where Freemasonry is practised and where temperatures in a Lodge room can get quite high, it makes sense to have a break in proceedings to allow Brethren to take a break and refresh themselves.

Collars

Today, we have collars of light blue, garter blue and red. Light blue is for the officers of a Lodge and Past Masters, whilst those of garter blue are for Provincial, District or Grand Officers. Red is for Provincial or Grand Stewards.

The Lodge officer's collar may be adorned with a chain; however, this is usually confined to a Master's collar. All chains worn in Masonic Lodges have to be approved by the Grand Lodge and must be placed down the centre of collar.

How did collars come about? In the early days of Freemasonry, and not until 1727 in fact, there was no standard design of a collar, because collars as we know them today were not worn. Instead the jewel of office was suspended from a ribbon or cord.

In June 1727, Grand Lodge resolved that the jewels were to be suspended from a white ribbon. No particular width of ribbon was specified at the time; however, by 1731 we begin to see some form of regulation, when Grand Lodge specified that the Grand Master, his Deputy and his Wardens were entitled to wear blue ribbons. The Grand Stewards wore red and the Master and Wardens of an ordinary Lodge wore white. At this time it would appear that nothing was specified for the other officers of a Lodge.

Grand Officer dress collar   Grand Officer undress collar
Courtesy Derek Hunt

Frederick Smyth, in his book A Reference Book for Freemasons, states: 'The earliest development of a (usually) narrow ribbon into the tailored and embellished article of clothing of today may well be attributable to France, where an exposure of 1742 describes the 'cordon' as 'taille en triangle', thus implying some sort of cutting to shape.'

The standard 4-inch-wide collar of today was only introduced after the Union of the two Grand Lodges in 1813, when most of our present-day regalia was standardised. As one progresses along the paths of Freemasonry, the collars become more elaborate with rank; for example, the Past Master's light blue collar is distinguished by a silver cord down the centre. Provincial and District Grand Officers have garter blue with gold edging for undress and gold fringe for full dress. Grand Officers' full dress collars are heavily embroidered with the sprig of Acacia and the Olive branch, whilst the undress is plain garter blue with no gold edging.

An officer of a Lodge should wear the collar of his office; however, if he holds two offices - which is the maximum he may hold (one regular and one additional office) - he may wear both collars. If he is a Past Master who holds a 'regular' office and an 'additional' one, he may wear his PM's collar with the other two on top. However, for practical purposes he should perhaps only wear the collar of the regular office.

Grand Stewards' collars are red and are four inches wide, whilst those of Provincial or District Stewards are also red but two inches wide.

There are other slight variations for three of the London Lodges where the officers of Lodges 3, 4 and 12 are permitted to wear a garter blue stripe on the centre of the collar.

Officers are permitted to wear their collars only in their own Lodge. The Master of a Lodge may only wear his collar outside his Lodge on special occasions such as a Provincial or District Grand Lodge meeting or when granted permission to do so by the Grand Master.

Dispensations

From time to time, we will hear the Worshipful Master say to the Secretary of a Lodge: 'Bro Secretary, will you please read the Dispensation'. He will then read a rather lengthy document couched in somewhat legalised language from the Provincial, District or Metropolitan Grand Master.

A dispensation gives a Lodge permission to do something which is not the 'norm'. For example, it may be to change the date of a meeting, the location, or both. There are also other dispensations, such as a candidate who has not yet achieved the age of

21 years. Or it may be that the Lodge has more than two candidates for a degree ceremony when the Lodge must also specify which degree ceremony will be conferred.

The Master of a Lodge may not continue in office for more than two years unless by dispensation and a Brother may not be the Master of more than two Lodges at the same time without a dispensation.

An unusual dispensation is the requirement for the proprietor or manager of a tavern or house where a Lodge meets to hold office in the Lodge. This stems back to the time when practically all Lodges met in an inn or tavern in which the landlord would normally be barred from holding office or becoming Master.

Regulation 178 states: 'No Brother shall appear clothed in any jewels, collars or badges of the Craft, in any procession, meeting or assemblage at which persons other than Masons are present, or in place of public resort, unless the Grand Master, or the Provincial or District Grand Master, as the case may be, has previously given a dispensation for Brethren to be there present in Masonic clothing.'

A Lodge may call an emergency meeting, for which a dispensation is required; however, there are restrictions on the type of business the Lodge may discuss. It is restricted to the business for which the emergency meeting was called - and no other - and the business to be discussed must be stated on the summons calling the meeting. No previous minutes will be read or confirmed at an emergency meeting except where such minutes relate to, or affect, the validity of the business stated.

Should the Treasurer of a Lodge become ill or his absence be of a protracted duration, a Lodge may, by dispensation, elect a member who is not serving a regular office in the Lodge to discharge the duties of the Treasurer until the actual Treasurer is able to resume his normal duties, or until the next regular period of election, whichever should occur first.

Finally, Regulation 109 states that if a Warden is not invested at the meeting at which a Master was installed and thereby the member appointed has not served in office for one full year, he cannot be among those eligible for election as Master of the Lodge, except by dispensation - and the circumstances which prevented him from being invested, the reason as to why it was delayed and the service of the member in the Warden's chair must be submitted as a petition for intervention by the Provincial or District Grand Master, as the case may be.

Free and Accepted Masons

The origin of the term is not fully known, but there is a reference in Latin as early as 1391 from Oxford: 'Master Mason of Free-stone'. So the term 'Freemason' may have emanated from this time. By the 17th century, the term 'Free-mason' (two words), had emerged and this term was in use at the time of Elias Ashmole's Initiation in Warrington in 1646.

There are various reasons given for the use of the word 'Free'. It has been used to describe those who worked in and sculpted free-stone, which was fine-grained sandstone or limestone which lent itself to easy carving and sculpture. This was suitable for carving window frames and doors, capitals and other ornamentation of largely Gothic buildings such as Cathedrals and Minsters.

Another use of the word 'free' applied to a man who was free to work on his own, having completed his indentures. He was then free to be made a 'Freeman' of the Borough or City. There are records from York which show that to be a member of one of the local guilds you had to be a Freeman.

Another explanation that has been put forward, particularly in American Masonry, is that the candidate was a 'free-man' and not a slave.

Anyone who was born outside a marriage, i.e. illegitimately born, would not be regarded as free and in the superstitious 1700s and in the Old Manuscript Charges they required a prospective apprentice to be of 'honest parentage' or 'to come of good kindred'. Today, in this age of anti-discrimination the latter would not be acceptable and the Craft is opposed to anything of this kind. But who might not be a 'freeman' today in terms being acceptable to Freemasonry?

Actually, we need look no further than Form P, the application form to join a Lodge. It asks the question: 'Have you been convicted of any criminal offence for which you have received a custodial sentence?' This in effect means that any such person is therefore not 'free' to become a Mason.

The term 'Accepted' comes from those who came into Freemasonry as gentlemen or non-operative members, those who did not actually engage in the stonemason's trade. In the Masons Company of London there are records which show the *'making of a Mason'* or *'coming on the Acception'*.

One example is when two Army Generals were 'accepted' into a Scottish Lodge meeting at Newcastle upon Tyne in 1641. Neither had any connection with the stonemason's craft. This, incidentally, is the earliest record of anyone being initiated into Freemasonry on English soil.

However, Ashmole's English record still stands, as they were initiated into a Scottish Lodge when the Scottish army invaded England. This was later confirmed in Lodge St. Mary's minutes in Edinburgh.

One other explanation, and one which I think is more likely, is that a man is free in his mind and wishes to become a Mason, as the ritual states 'freedom of inclination'. In my view that is the true meaning of the term 'Free'.

Gauntlets

Gauntlets were originally long-sleeved gloves, worn from medieval times by knights, workmen and others who had a need to protect their wrists and forearms as well as their hands.

If you look at old photographs of Masons wearing gauntlets you might see that they are extended gloves and of a one-piece construction. In the Masonic sense they have long since ceased to exist and today the gauntlets we wear in our Lodges are represented by the simple white glove with an extension of a tapering tube of stiffened material with a badge of office embroidered on the outside.

At one time, there were certain Lodges where all officers wore gauntlets of the one-piece type, but today only the Master and the two Wardens wear the modern type in English Constitution Lodges.

These are described in the *Book of Constitutions* for private Lodges as light blue silk with silver embroidery with the emblem of office within a double circle, usually with the name and number of the Lodge.

For Grand Officers they are to be of Garter blue silk with gold embroidery and for Provincial and District Grand Officers Garter blue with gold lace embroidery and gold emblems. For Provincial and District Grand Stewards, red silk with silver emblems.

Graham Redman in his book *Masonic Etiquette Today* has this to say:

> *'Because of the elaborate embroidery, gauntlets are an expensive item and they ceased to be mandatory part of a Grand and Provincial Grand Officers dress in 1971 when the Board of General Purposes examined the historical background to their wearing and concluded: 'that their use as separate items of regalia is derived rather from a change of fashion and as a matter of convenience, than from any real symbolic significance.'*

They have long since ceased to be worn by officers of the year in Grand Lodge.

There are only a few Provinces now, such as West Lancashire, where gauntlets are worn regularly as a matter of course. Everywhere else their use has been abandoned.

Gloves

You might ask: Why do we wear white gloves? Actually we do not *need* to, it is up to the Master to decide whether the members of his Lodge wear gloves or not.

In many Lodges - and I am a member of one where gloves are not worn - it was decided that it should be that way at the consecration of the Lodge and has remained so ever since.

Gloves have always carried a certain symbolism, even from the Middle Ages, in military, legal and court circles, and in our case, along with the white lambskin apron, they are symbols of innocence and purity of heart. We also know that employers provided masons with gloves in addition to their wages. For instance the records of York Minster c. 1335, show that masons were provided with gowns, aprons, gloves and clogs.

However, their use today in Masonic Lodges is controlled by Grand Lodge. An extract from the Board of GP minutes of 10 June 1964:

Grand Lodge Regulations state:

> *'It is left to the discretion of the Master of each Lodge to decide, after considering the interests of members generally, whether to request that they should be worn.*

The Board considers that when such a request is made it should cover all present and not as sometimes occurs, the Officers of the Lodge only.

The Board recommends the Grand Lodge to rule that if gloves are to be worn they should be worn at all times except:

By candidates for the three degrees
By the Master Elect when actually taking his Obligation on the VSL.

Gloves would thus not be removed by the Master (or Wardens or temporary occupants of their chairs or by any other Brother assisting them) in the course of entrusting or examining candidates, or when investing Officers.

The Board sees no objection to Entered Apprentices and Fellow Crafts wearing gloves when not actually being passed or raised.'

It is usually printed on a Lodge summons if white gloves are to be worn.

Why the ungloved hand during the obligation? In the Masonic exposure *Masonry Dissected 1730,* during the obligation a candidate speaks of *'my naked right hand on the Holy Bible'.*

It therefore makes sense that nothing should intervene between the human hand and the Volume of the Sacred Law when a solemn obligation is being taken.

Grand Officers

What is a Grand Officer? Who are they and what do they do? To a less experienced Mason their status is not very clear. Let us take a look at what it says in the *Book of Constitutions; General Laws and Regulations:*

The Grand Lodge.

'*Reg. 2. The interests of the Fraternity are managed by a general representation of all private Lodges on the Register, The Grand Stewards for the year and the Grand Officers, present and past, with the Grand Master at their head. This collective body is styled THE UNITED GRAND LODGE OF ANTIENT FREE AND ACCEPTED MASONS OF ENGLAND hereinafter referred to as "The Grand Lodge".*'

Now that does not tell us a great deal, but Reg. 5 then ranks the Grand Officers in order, starting with the Grand Master and ends with the 84th which are The Master, Past Masters and Wardens of Grand Stewards Lodge and of every other private Lodge.

The first Grand Officers did not appear until eighteen years after the formation of the first Grand Lodge of 1717, except for the Grand Master, his Deputy and two Wardens who had been in place since its inception.

Craft Grand Officer's full dress regalia – apron and gauntlets. *Courtesy Derek Hunt*

Craft Grand Officer – undress apron.
Courtesy Derek Hunt

English Freemasonry is a hierarchical system in private Lodges as well as in Provincial and District Grand Lodges and Grand Lodge. The introduction of different Grand ranks emerged over a long period of time with the present list being generally formed in 1813 at the merger of the two Grand Lodges. There is Acting Grand Rank and there are Past Grand Ranks. Acting Ranks and Past Ranks are appointed annually with certain exceptions, for example: The Grand Master and Grand Treasurer must be nominated and elected annually. The Grand Secretary and the Grand Tyler hold their appointments during the Grand Master's pleasure.

Acting or Past Grand Officer rank is given for the purpose of recognising long, faithful and especially valuable service to the Craft. Many who receive it will have either held positions of responsibility in a Provincial Grand Lodge, such as Provincial Grand Secretary, Charity Steward or Provincial Almoner or taken charge of a Group, District or area and it is generally given for outstanding service. The process of recommendation and selection are tried and tested and are operated with all possible impartiality. The appointments take place annually at the April Quarterly Communications of Grand Lodge in London.

Grand Officers have their own regalia, consisting of full dress which is quite ornate and undress which is plain and worn at ordinary Lodge meetings. The full dress regalia is worn for Lodge Installations or other special occasions, such as a 50th celebration or a Lodge centenary. Illustrations of their regalia can be found in *The Book of Constitutions.*

Frequently, and especially in larger Provinces, a Grand Officer will 'represent' a Provincial Grand Master at the Installation of a Master of a Lodge. He is there to act on behalf of the Provincial Grand Master and will often convey the messages the PGM wishes to pass on to his Lodges. They also take a lead in local affairs and on account of their experience will often be consulted for their advice.

In other Constitutions, such as Ireland and Scotland, they also have Grand Officers but the arrangements for the appointment of Grand Officers are quite different to the English system and too complex to describe in a paper of this length. A visit to their Grand Lodge websites may provide you with this information.

Heart, Hand, Badge Sign

This is usually given during the Installation ceremony by Fellowcrafts on their return to the Lodge. Where does it come from and what is its significance?

I do not believe it is a 'sign' as it is often referred to, but rather a salutation. Harry Carr in *Freemason at Work* states: '*The sign was described in two old documents of 1700 and 1711. In those days it only partially resembled our present day F.C. sign which is a much expanded version.*'

In the Masonic Exposure of 1760, '*Three Distinct Knocks*' it is described as: '*holding your left hand up, keeping it square; then clap with your right hand and left together, and from thence strike your left breast with your right hand; then strike your apron, and your right foot going at the same time. This is done together as one clap.*'

Harry Carr asks: '*Why in the Installation and not elsewhere?*' and answers: '*I suggest it is because the Fellowcraft, from time immemorial, was the essential degree during Installation. Masters were chosen from the Fellowcrafts in the days when only two degrees existed and long before the Installation Ceremony had come into practice, and to this day the Master Elect takes his Obligation in the F.C. Degree.*'

Since Harry Carr wrote that, I have discovered that at least one Lodge in the very large Province of West Lancashire uses it outside of the Installation ceremony as a salutation to a newly appointed Provincial Officer, if in the Second Degree.

Incidentally, the Installation ceremony did not exist in the Moderns Grand Lodge before the Union, but it did exist in the Antients Grand Lodge and therefore it is likely that '*The Three Distinct Knocks*' was referring to the practice of an Antients Lodge.

What is the correct sequence? Actually, it varies across the United Kingdom. For some it is Heart, Apron, Glove, in others it is known as the Breast, Hand, Badge. In Bristol it is given Hand, Breast, Badge and in Lancashire as the Hand, Heart, Badge sign.

The Duke of Sussex set up a special Lodge or Board of Installed Masters to revise and standardise the Installation ceremony, which had not been done at the time of the Union in 1813. A minute from this Lodge, which is the only official reference referring to the salutation, reads 'Sal: Br; ha; ba;' obviously from the sequence described, and despite an attempt by this Lodge, it has never become standardised.

Whatever the actual sequence, I cannot resist a comment on the appalling misuse of this salutation at some Installation ceremonies. Often it is done far too quickly to be meaningful, and can often be seen degenerating into a shambles with Brethren getting completely out of synchronisation. If I may bring one appeal to the Directors of Ceremonies amongst us, please do it at a pace which allows the Brethren to follow the sequence in a proper manner.

Hints and Tips for the New Mason

In no particular order.

Always practise your salutes as you go through your degrees. A good salute always impresses. Ask your Lodge Mentor, Proposer or Seconder if you are not sure what to do.

Be aware that you will be required to leave the Lodge and give a salute when the Lodge moves to a higher degree for which you are not yet qualified.

Also the same applies when you are returning into the Lodge; you will be met by the DC or ADC and you will take a step and salute the WM before taking your seat. The DC will advise you of the salute to give.

Make sure your apron is tight enough around your waist and not hanging down like a dishcloth around your knees! A good tip is to ensure that the belt or strings are above your jacket pockets; that way it is less likely to slide down.

If you are unable to attend your meetings for any reason, *always* inform the Secretary and give your apologies.

Do not be afraid to ask questions; everybody is willing to help you. Your Proposer, Seconder or Mentor will try and answer any query you may have. If they are unable to help they will find someone who can.
Learn the ritual of the next office above you as well as your current one.

Read the notice-boards in your Masonic Hall. Frequently there will be something advertised on there that will interest you.

If you arrive late for your Lodge you will be met by the DC or ADC and you will give a salute when you enter as before. A few words of apology are always advisable.

Be aware that when you are visiting another Lodge you may be asked to respond on behalf of visitors, but usually only if there are no more senior visiting Brethren present.

Although it is unlikely to happen, always be aware that if you are visiting a Lodge where you are not known, you may be requested to prove yourself. This will require you to be able to give the various passwords pertaining to any of the three degrees. Do remember them just in case. This is only likely to happen if the Brother who invited you is not present to prove who you are - and in any case it is always wise to have your GL certificate with you when visiting another Lodge.

If you have purchased a Provincial tie, please be aware that you may only wear it in your *own* Province. If you are visiting another Lodge which is outside your Province, you should wear a black tie or the Craft tie.

Pay your subscriptions on the day they are due or before if possible.

Remember that the more you put into Freemasonry, the more you will get out of it. Do a little and you will only receive a little.

Never allow a new Brother to sit in Lodge on his own; look after him and remember just how you felt when you first came into Freemasonry.

And finally one for us *all*...

Do not hold a conversation whilst Lodge business is being conducted. There is nothing detracts more from a good ceremony than Brethren talking loudly whilst it is in progress and it is bad manners to do so.

Honorary Membership

Rule 167 of The Book of Constitutions states: 'A Lodge shall have the power, after notice placed on the summons, to elect as an Honorary Member, any Brother of good standing and worthy of such distinction by reason of his services to the Craft, or to the particular Lodge, who is, or within the previous year has been, a subscribing member of a regular Lodge. The motion for his election shall be voted on by ballot and declared carried unless three or more black balls appear against it.'

It then goes on to state that he will have no voting rights in the Lodge unless he again becomes a subscribing member, but he has the right to attend any meeting of the Lodge.

If, however, the distinction of Honorary Membership has been conferred upon a Past Master because of the services he has rendered to the Lodge, he shall, if he has been a subscribing member thereof, be entitled to propose and second candidates for admission to the Lodge.

It should never be forgotten that Honorary Membership is a privilege and no one has a right to demand it. It should only be awarded to Brethren who have given *outstanding* service to the Craft or the Lodge in particular. The mere fact that someone has been a member of a Lodge for 'x' number of years may not be sufficient to warrant Honorary Membership, unless as it says, there has been outstanding service of some kind. Sometimes Honorary Membership may be given out too lightly and Lodge members should give very careful consideration to any suggestion of offering this honour.

Once a Brother is made an Honorary Member, he becomes an unattached Mason, if he is not a subscribing member of another Lodge. There are of course restrictions placed upon unattached Brethren in regard to visiting other Lodges. Also, he may not hold an office in his Lodge except that of Tyler (Rule 104b).

What if an Honorary Member decides to visit the Lodge that has so honoured him? Should he pay for his meal at the Festive Board? After all he does not pay a subscription any more. That is a matter for the Lodge to decide; however, etiquette would suggest that the Honorary Member should certainly expect to pay.

Can he invite a visitor to the Lodge? Actually, there is nothing to stop him doing so as long as the Lodge permits it; however, it should be at his own or his visitor's expense.

Many Lodges invite Consecrating Officers or other senior Brethren from their Province, such as the Provincial Grand Master, or his Deputy or Assistants to become Honorary Members - but it is not necessarily restricted to members of their own Constitution. It may also be offered to members of another Constitution which may have special connections with a Lodge.

Finally, always be careful who you invite to Honorary Membership. Remember, the honour is for a subscribing Brother in good standing; in other words, not in arrears with his Lodge and who is worthy of that distinction.

Landmarks

The words 'a Landmark in Freemasonry' are those that we often hear during the course of our Masonic ceremonies. But what are they? My bet is that if you ask a colleague he will not be able to tell you. The United Grand Lodge of England's *Book of Constitutions* only mentions Landmarks four times. Under Rule 4, The Grand Lodge possesses the supreme superintending authority etc....always taking care that the Ancient Landmarks of the Order be preserved.

> *Rule 55: (of irregular Propositions): If it shall appear to the Grand Master that any resolution contains anything contrary to the Antient Landmarks of the Order, he may refuse to permit the same to be discussed.*

> *Rule 111: Every Master Elect, before being placed in the Chair, shall solemnly pledge himself to preserve the Landmarks of the Order.*

> *Rule 125 (b) (related to the admission of visitors): it says, in part, that: No Brother shall be admitted unless...he has been initiated into a Lodge in which a belief in TGAOTU is professed, as this belief is an essential landmark of the Order.*

However, nowhere does it stipulate what the others are. The late Harry Carr considered the following:

> *'A landmark must have existed from the 'time whereof the memory of man runneth not to the contrary' and a landmark is an element in the form or essence of the Society of such importance that Freemasonry would no longer be Freemasonry if it were to be removed.'*

If these two qualifications are used strictly to test whether certain practices, systems, principles, or regulations can be admitted as Landmarks, it will be found that there are actually very few items that will pass this rigid test. Nevertheless, the tendency, even among prominent writers who try to compile lists of landmarks, seems to be to incorporate items which actually come under the heading of regulations or customs or principles, and tentative lists of landmarks range from five to fifty-odd separate items.

The following is suggested as a list of acceptable Landmarks which would conform to the two-point test:

That a Mason professes a belief in God (The Supreme Being), GAOTU.

That the VSL is an essential and indispensable part of the Lodge, to be open in full view when Brethren are at labour.

That a Mason must be male, free-born, of mature age and of good character.

That a Mason, by his Tenure, owes allegiance to the Sovereign and to the Craft.

That a Mason believes in the immortality of the soul.

The first four on the list are derived from the Ancient Charges. Robert Macoy, in his *Dictionary of Freemasonry* states:

> 'Of the nature of the landmarks of Masonry, there has been some diversity of opinion; yet the conviction has become settled that the true principles constituting landmarks are those universal customs of the Order which have gradually grown into permanent rules of action, and originally established by competent authority, at a period so remote that no account of their origin is to be found in the records of Masonic history and which were considered essential to the preservation and integrity of the institution, to preserve its purity and prevent innovation.'

Finally, many Grand Lodges, especially in the USA, have listed landmarks from as few as 3 to 54 and Macoy settled for 25. My view as an English Mason is inclined to side with Harry Carr.

Lodge Amalgamation

It is not uncommon, especially in some of the larger provinces, for Lodges to amalgamate. The reasons for this can be varied; they may be brought about by an ageing membership or a general lack of interest and resignations - or even internal squabbles leading to disruption and decline. Sometimes the membership of a Lodge will decline the opportunity to amalgamate, when numbers are low, preferring to hand in the Lodge Warrant and close.

A Lodge must have a minimum of five members and should its membership fall below that number the Lodge shall cease to exist. (Rule 188 *Book of Constitutions.*) However, the need to amalgamate or for a Lodge to hand in its Warrant will occur long before such low numbers are reached.

The usual amalgamation will consist of two Lodges, a strong one and a weaker Lodge, but it is not unknown for three or even four Lodges to come together. The usual criterion is the size of membership; for instance two Lodges with, for example, 12 members each would be unlikely to be able to obtain approval to amalgamate, whereas a Lodge with 40 members and a Lodge with 15 would most likely receive approval.

Before amalgamation takes place there are usually several meetings to be held between the interested parties to decide which shall be the prevailing Lodge, i.e. the Lodge which will retain its Warrant. The other Lodge(s) will have their Warrant(s) endorsed by Grand Lodge and their name(s) removed from the list of Lodges. Under Rule 102a, the Grand Master may - at his discretion and upon such conditions as he shall see fit - grant a Certificate of Amalgamation. Provincial or District officials will be involved at a very early stage to offer guidance and advice to ensure that negotiations run smoothly.

Many things need to be settled between the parties before the formal merger, such as the name of the new Lodge. There is also the matter of Lodge finances and bank accounts to be resolved, also Lodge possessions such as artefacts, and what will happen to them at the amalgamation. There will also be the question of the mode of working. Often Lodges will have slight differences in their procedures and this must be considered and agreed by both parties beforehand. One of the major considerations is who will do what when two or more Lodges come together. Who are going to be the officers of the new Lodge? All these matters need to be ironed out and it may take several months and many meetings before a final agreement is reached.

Do amalgamations work? Some do and some don't. My own personal experience of being a member of an amalgamated Lodge has been a very positive one; however, it does not happen by itself and a lot of hard work and tolerance is needed to make it successful. It is not unknown for mergers to fail because of the intransigence of some members.

I have also experienced a situation where two relatively small Lodges (of 15 and 20 members) who would not have received agreement to formally merge have successfully devised a means of working together to their mutual advantage. How did this work? Well, both Lodges agreed to reduce the number of their meetings from nine per year to five and each shared the work and retained their own Master. A pattern was required to work out their meetings, which would require each Lodge to have an election meeting followed by its Installation. In this instance a fifth meeting was a joint meeting with both Lodges opening and closing on the same evening.

The Warrant of an amalgamated Lodge will be put on display at meetings of the new Lodge along with the Warrant(s) of the subsumed Lodge(s) also being displayed. If a Hall Stone jewel belongs to one of the Lodges it will continue to be worn by the Master of the new Lodge.

Lodge Names

Under Rule 98 of the English Constitution, all Lodges are required to have a name and these are many and varied. All are followed by a number. A Lodge may not make any alteration to its name without the prior approval of the Grand Master, or in a Metropolitan area, Province or District, without that of the Metropolitan, Provincial, or District Grand Masters of those areas.

Some are named after an Order of Architecture such as Tuscan, Doric or Corinthian. Others are named after the four cardinal virtues Prudence, Justice, Temperance and Fortitude and the theological virtues Faith, Hope and Charity.

Many saints' names are used. A common one is St. John, named after the two saints associated with Freemasonry, i.e. St. John the Baptist, celebrated on 24 June and St. John the Evangelist celebrated on 27 December. Very often an Installation meeting will be named The Festival of St. John.

Other names may be place names, e.g. Orrell, and these are very common. Some are named after prominent individuals, e.g. Earl of Lathom Lodge, and many are very short, such as Oak. But there are numerous longer names such as True Light Lodge of Friendship of Warrington. The longest name I can find is the District Grand Stewards Lodge of Jamaica and the Cayman Islands with 53 letters and the shortest, Wa Lodge in Ghana with just two.

In Ireland, however, as many as ninety Lodges have no name and are simply numbered. Others under that Constitution have names in a similar manner to English Lodges.

In Scotland it is normal practice to give the name of the Lodge as, for example, Lodge St. Clair No. 427, whereas in England we say, for example, Sincerity Lodge, unless the name specifies it otherwise - such as The Lodge of Faith.

In Scotland, for example, it is Lodge Forbes followed by the number. The word *of* is rarely used.

In the USA, Lodge names follow a similar form to that used in England.

Graham Redman, Assistant Grand Secretary, in his book *Masonic Etiquette Today* comments that the Grand Master's advisers are unwilling to support the naming of a Lodge which is that of a living or deceased Freemason under the rank of Metropolitan, Provincial or District Grand Master. However, they may be willing to support a name which is that of a famous person (not necessarily a Freemason or even a man) who is dead, e.g. Sir Edward Elgar Lodge No. 9837.

Lodge Warrants

Let us take a look at what the *Book of Constitutions* says about Lodge Warrants:

> *'Except under the provisions of Rule 95, no Lodge may meet without a warrant of constitution from the Grand Master, which is to be specially entrusted to each Master at his installation, to be held by him in safe custody on behalf of the Grand Master. The Master shall produce it at every meeting of the Lodge.'*

Note, Brethren: *'Shall produce it at every meeting of the Lodge'* - it does not say *display* it at every meeting. However, it must be shown to a candidate at his Initiation. It is the responsibility of the Master of a Lodge - not the Secretary - to ensure its safekeeping.

In some Constitutions, the Warrant will be present at the meeting but not necessarily displayed and may remain rolled up, perhaps in the tube it is stored in. In fact, I know of one English Craft Lodge which does just that at every meeting. In many instances, Lodge Warrants will be on permanent display on the walls of a Lodge room.

The Warrant of a Lodge is the property of the Grand Master and it must be retained for the sole use of the Lodge to which it is granted. A Warrant may not have any endorsement or inscription except with the authority of the Grand Master.

What if the Warrant was lost, for instance in a fire or flood? Then the Lodge must suspend its meetings until a Warrant of Confirmation has been issued by the Grand Master. If the Warrant was recovered then the Warrant of Confirmation should be returned.

When were Warrants first issued? Well, according to Frederick Smyth in his book *A Reference Book for Freemasons* the first Warrants were not issued until 1731 by the Grand Lodge of England of 1717. Prior to this time, a Lodge would meet with a copy of one of the Old Charges present. There is some evidence to support this as Edward Sankey was requested to make a copy of an Old Charge on the day the Initiation of Elias Ashmole took place at Warrington in October 1646. His father, Richard, was one of those present at the Initiation ceremony.

However, there are some Lodges which still meet today without a Warrant. They are the Grand Steward's Lodge which has no number and the three old 'Time Immemorial Lodges'. They are Antiquity No. 2, Royal Somerset House and Inverness No. 4 and the Lodge of Fortitude and Old Cumberland No. 12. Royal Navy Lodge No. 59, which has existed since 1739, meets without any official authority although it does not have the designation 'Time Immemorial'.

In the USA a 'Warrant' is known as a Charter, as it is in New Zealand and Canada and some other Constitutions.

There are other Warrants issued by United Grand Lodge, in addition to the two already mentioned. These are Centenary Warrants, which entitle the members of a Lodge to wear a Centenary jewel, and Bi-Centenary Warrants. It is not proper to produce only a Centenary Warrant at a meeting as it does not supersede the original Warrant, so both must be present when a meeting takes place.

Masonic Charity

At every Lodge meeting there is a collection for charity - a tradition that goes back a long, long way. Charity is one of the basic principles of Freemasonry and has existed since the earliest days of the Order, particularly after the formation of the first Grand Lodge in 1717, after which the number of Lodges increased considerably. Prior to this time, charitable giving would appear to have been on a casual relief basis according to need.

What is known is that in those early days charity was practised. In 1722 Joshua Timson, a Grand Warden, was given assistance and by November 1724 there was indeed a petition for help in Grand Lodge for the first Grand Master Anthony Sayer who had fallen on hard times. This petition was approved. Further sums were voted for him in 1730 and 1741.

Formalising charity giving by Lodges took place in 1726 when a committee to administer charity was founded and the first contributions by private Lodges were received in 1729. The Committee of Charity was permitted on proper examination to give relief to petitioners of up to five guineas. Anything above that amount had to be approved by Grand Lodge.

By 1733, the brief of the Committee of Charity was broadened to include the business of the Quarterly Communications and matters pertaining to the administration of the Craft. This continued in the Moderns Grand Lodge until the merger in 1813. A similar arrangement was set up by the Antients Grand Lodge after that had been formed in 1752. By 1799, a Masonic Benefit Society had been set up; however, it proved so popular that claims outweighed its assets and income and it had to be wound up.

The beginnings of two of the major Masonic charities arose in the late eighteenth century, those of the Royal Masonic Institute for Girls and the Royal Masonic Institute for Boys, two of the four major Masonic charitable institutions. These have now become the Royal Masonic Trust for Girls & Boys.

By 1830 it had been suggested that a benevolent institution should be formed and Dr. Robert Crucifix advocated the setting up of an Asylum for Aged and Decaying Freemasons. This did not meet with the approval of Grand Lodge, but despite this lack of formal approval the Asylum project went ahead. Grand Lodge was, however, not to be outdone and set up the Royal Masonic Benevolent Annuity Fund. Eventually they merged in 1850, to become the Royal Masonic Benevolent Institution for Aged Freemasons and their Widows, now known as the Royal Masonic Benevolent Institution (RMBI). They now have no fewer than 18 homes located throughout the country.

The fourth major Masonic charity is the Masonic Samaritan Fund founded in 1990, which exists to fund the provision of medical care and support for Freemasons, the wives and dependants of Freemasons and the widows, partners and dependants of deceased Freemasons.

Finally there is the Freemasons Grand Charity which was established in 1961. It gives donations to Masonic and non-Masonic charities and has been responsible for donations over the past 10 years running into millions of pounds and is probably the largest donor to charity in the UK after the National Lottery Fund and Children in Need.

Masonic Dress, Ties and Lapel Pins

Masonic dress and ties can sometimes be an emotive thing. Pride in one's Province and the desire to show that you are a member of it is understandable; however, incorrect use can also occasionally cause offence.

Let us take a look at what the *Book of Constitutions* has to say on the matter: '*Brethren will no doubt have noticed that instructions for Masonic functions held under the auspices of the Grand Lodge indicate that dark clothing, black tie and white collar should be worn...etc.*'

Today, in Lodges of the English Constitution, the norm is a dark coloured lounge suit. Black, charcoal or grey suit are the norm with dark jacket and striped trousers for Provincial and Grand Officers if they wish, a white shirt and black tie. Whilst this is acceptable for most Lodges, others require their officers to wear an evening suit at all meetings and some wear an evening suit at all meetings or at Installations only. There are also other modes of dress which I will come to later.

As Graham Redman, the Assistant Grand Secretary in his book *Masonic Etiquette Today* advises: '*It goes - or should go - without saying that a member of a Lodge should be careful to conform to the dress code it has adopted. A visitor also should, as a part of the courtesy that is one of the reciprocal obligations of hospitality, conform if he is able, - and if he is not, should at least show sensitivity to the customs of his hosts.'*

There are some university Lodges where it is the custom to wear their gowns over their regalia and there are at least two who wear court dress (i.e. knee breeches, black silk stockings and buckled shoes, white tie and waistcoat, with evening tailcoat or a variant of that dress. In some military Lodges it is the norm for the members to wear mess kit or full uniform (instead of morning dress).

Highland dress, however, can be more of a problem and it normally requires the permission of the Provincial Grand Master to allow the wearing of this type of attire by expatriate Scots or those of Scots descent. It should *not* be assumed, however, that it is acceptable when visiting another Lodge.

In respect of ties, this is a controversial area and often Brethren are confused as to what they may or may not wear in a Craft Lodge. Let us take a look: plain black tie – always acceptable. Craft tie – likewise, always acceptable Black ties bearing an emblem, whether in the weave or printed, are *not* acceptable. An absolute 'no-no' is a tie associated with another Order.

But what about Provincial ties?

Members of a particular Metropolitan area, Province or District are encouraged to wear their particular tie within their area. However, they should not be worn when visiting a Lodge in another area, unless the Metropolitan, Provincial or District Grand Master of that area has given his permission. A visitor to another area should not presume that such permission has been given and it is courtesy to avoid the wearing of such ties in these circumstances.

Certain ties are acceptable, however, when associated with a regiment, college, school or livery, but only within those associations. There are also various groupings of Lodges such as the Kindred Lodges Association or the Athol Lodges Association who have particular ties which may be worn only at meetings of those Associations.

If in doubt, always wear either a plain black tie or the Craft tie and you won't go wrong. However, wearing a tie half undone, as is frequently seen these days, is also unacceptable. What we do outside Freemasonry as a fashion statement is not necessarily acceptable inside.

With regard to lapel pins, the answer is simple. Those associated with other Orders should not be worn in a Craft Lodge under any circumstances.

Masonic Imposters

Has it ever crossed your mind, when you have visited another Lodge outside your own area and having entered the Lodge with little or no checks being carried out in regard to your credentials, whether someone with enough knowledge of Freemasonry and a bit of regalia could get into a meeting as an imposter? Well it may surprise you to know that Masonic imposters were a major problem right across English and American Masonry in the late 1800s and into the early 20th century.

In the English Craft today, we very rarely test a visitor to see if he is *bona fide*. In Scotland, however, it is normal practice to ensure that a visitor is a true and worthy Brother by taking him aside into a room where two or more Past Masters will put him through an examination and then follow this up by declaring him so tested in open Lodge, before he is admitted.

Such was the problem during the period mentioned that one Brother decided to do his bit to put a stop to it. He was James Pownall, a PM and Secretary of a Lodge in Ashton-under-Lyne, Lancashire, and the Sub-Almoner for eight Lodges in the Province of East Lancashire and five in nearby Cheshire. The system at the time was very unlike the current one with a mixture of Lodge Almoners, Sub-Almoners and District Almoners. A Sub-Almoner was

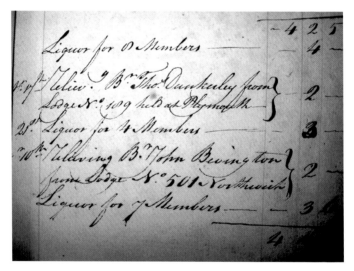

An entry from the cash book of the Lodge of Sincerity No. 492 in 1792 showing 2/- cash being paid to a Thomas Dunkerley as charity relief. The lodge in Plymouth didn't exist and it is likely that this was a case of a Masonic impostor.

in charge of several Lodges and a District Almoner for Lodges in a particular geographical area. There was no overall Grand Lodge control as there is now through Masonic charities.

In the late 1800s, there was a considerable number of men travelling around the country soliciting alms from Lodge Almoners, with cases being reported right across England from Cornwall to Cumbria. According to Bro. Pownall, around fifty different individuals were known to be falsely claiming relief. His investigations uncovered men who used numerous aliases and he drew attention to the fact that he had discovered one man who was using twelve different names, two others with nine, two with seven, three with five, three with four and several with three and two. He also compiled a list of some 230 cases right across the country. Not all tried visiting a Lodge meeting; some were former Masons and others complete imposters, who, armed with some knowledge, would prey on unsuspecting Almoners, claiming relief.

Some were even 'plying their trade' across the Atlantic and there are several cases of false claims in New York, Chicago and other cities by 'vagrants' who were doing a similar thing as in England.

Although there were numerous prosecutions and several men were jailed for periods of up to three months with hard labour for obtaining money by false pretences, it caused a dilemma for the Craft. Among many 'well esteemed' Brethren there was a view that to prosecute these men was 'very degrading to our Order'. However, two Masonic magazines at the time, *The Freemason* and *The Freemason's Chronicle* strongly supported the action of prosecution. They even went so far as to suggest to the authorities that a central organisation should be set up, similar to the Masonic Association of America which had been highly successful in reducing this kind of abuse.

Brother Pownall was a very determined individual and he single-handedly produced a list of names, with photographs in some cases, of the known impostors, together with hints and suggestions for Almoners. This was circulated widely across the country, resulting in many more prosecutions. Because of this it became harder and harder for 'masonic vagrants' to make false claims for charity and cases eventually died out.

Masonic Obligations

Every Freemason takes a solemn obligation on the Volume of the Sacred Law when he enters the Craft - but *why*?

To answer the question, let us take a look at an Obligation and an Oath. In *Chambers Dictionary*, an Obligation is described as: *'the act of obliging; a moral or legal bond, tie, or binding power; an action, promise or requirement of such a kind that failure to perform or fulfil it contravenes the law; the thing to which one is bound; a debt of gratitude; a favour; a bond containing a penalty in case of failure.'*

That is a very comprehensive definition and not all of it applies to Masonry of course; however, I would argue that there is not much which does not. The only parts I would exclude are '*a debt of gratitude*' and '*a favour*'. Of course, the law to which we are referring is Masonic Law and a penalty in case of failure is purely a symbolic one in the Masonic sense.

An Oath, on the other hand, is not quite so strong and in *Chambers* it is defined as: '*a solemn appeal to a god or something holy or reverenced as witness or sanction of the truth of a statement; the form of words used; a more or less similar expression used lightly, exclamatorily, decoratively, or in imprecation, a swear-word, a curse.'*

So there is a subtle difference between the two. To put it briefly, an oath can be defined as a solemn appeal to a deity to witness one's determination to keep a promise, whereas an obligation is a binding moral, legal and even spiritual agreement. The derivation of the word itself is from the Latin *'obligare'* meaning to bind or tie.

How long have we been using Obligations in the Masonic sense? Well, we can certainly go back to the Old Charges, for instance the Regius Poem of 1390, although it refers to an oath (in modern English):

> '*And shall swear the same oat*
> *Of the Masons,*
> *Be they willing be they loth…'*

The Worshipful Society of Freemasons of London had an obligation which was written in 1686 by the Clerk to the Society, Robert Padgett. In the Antients Grand Lodge a candidate would take his obligation, kneeling at a central altar with one hand flat under the VSL and the other on top of it, a custom which many will recognise from the Grand Lodge of Scotland as the Due Guard.

The importance of an obligation cannot be overlooked, for what binds Freemasons together is the fact that they have all taken a solemn obligation. Its significance is not so much in the words but in what they convey to the candidate in his heart: that he should not break his word once having taken that obligation.

Do you remember the words at the end of the initiate's obligation: '*You will be branded a wilfully perjured individual void of all moral worth…*'? It is a Freemason's integrity which is being tested by that obligation, and we must always remember that the obligation makes us reflect upon what his word is worth, not just to other Freemasons but to all men at all times.

Masonic Symbolism

To do justice to the topic of Masonic symbolism would take far more than a mere short paper such as this. Symbolism in Freemasonry is everywhere; much of it has evolved over time. A lot of it is intentional and deliberately inserted into our ritual because it conveys a message to the recipient.

As to the origins of symbolism in Masonry, that is an unknown question; we simply do not know when and where it was first used, but a clue might be in the following by that famous historian Douglas Knoop. Talking of the Old Charges he said:

> 'In a century in which allegorical interpretation of the scriptures was commonly practised, as is shown, for example by the publication in 1688 of John Bunyan's Solomon's Temple Spiritualised, it would not be surprising to find that the use of allegory was introduced into Freemasonry at that period.'

He went on to say that symbolism which suffered a temporary eclipse following the Reformation but was being made use of by the Anglicans before the end of the 16th century and by the Puritans somewhat later, came to be generally regarded with favour in the 17th century and it is therefore easy to understand why its use might have been adopted by speculative Masons in teaching the principles for which Freemasonry stood.

The Initiate is told that Freemasonry is *a peculiar system of morality, veiled in allegory and illustrated by symbols*. But the world is full of symbols; you only have to enter an airport to see the overwhelming use of symbols. However, they are not a modern thing and are not exclusive to Freemasonry. Man has been using them for hundreds of years, from the dawn of creation. Early man drew an image of a bison on the wall of his cave using charcoal, perhaps to symbolise his prowess as a great hunter. We are told by historians that the initial learning by human beings was done through symbols. The Christian Church used many symbols and they were used by the Egyptians before that, as witnessed by the elaborate hieroglyphics on the walls of their tombs and other buildings.

Harry Carr in *The Freemason at Work* offers a good explanation of symbolism:

'Symbols are a mode of communication; they teach by implication, or recollection, or interpretation. But symbolism is not an exact science. So far as I know, there are no rules by which we can measure the authenticity, or logic, or accuracy of one's interpretation. Our estimation of truth or accuracy, in dealing with symbols, will be governed entirely by how far a particular explanation or interpretation is in accord with our own previous convictions, or how far it may succeed in satisfying us in our search for understanding.

'Hence I agree that every man is fully entitled (and should be encouraged) to work out his own symbolism and, when he has done this to his own satisfaction, his symbolism is valid for him, regardless of the arguments of extraneous logic…'

Must We Follow the Ritual to the Book?

This is a very good question - and one which has created discussion over many years. United Grand Lodge does not publish or authorise publication of any specific form of ritual, whether written, printed or spoken.

Prior to the Union of the two Grand Lodges of England in 1813, there was considerable difference of working between the two of them and even from Lodge to Lodge. However, when attempts were being made to bring the two Grand Lodges together, work was also going on behind the scenes to devise a form of ritual which was acceptable to both sides.

A Lodge of Promulgation was formed with members from both sides for this purpose. Their task was to study landmarks and esoteric matters and to make recommendations towards a suitable ritual. This was some five years before the eventual merger. Promulgation means 'to make widely known' and eventually a form of ritual emerged which we now know as 'Emulation'. Shortly before the Union, another Lodge was formed by dispensation of the two Grand Masters, The Lodge of Reconciliation, whose task was to disseminate the new ritual.

However, there was no published ritual and the new one had be passed by word of mouth by ritual experts whose task was to travel around demonstrating the new forms to Lodges up and down the country.

Although a remarkable degree of standardisation did take place, variations remained in different parts of the country, notably in Bristol and in the North-West of England, where many of the old practices remained.

I have been asked many times: *'How far can a Lodge deviate from Emulation as it is written down?'* Some argue that it cannot be changed and should follow the book to the letter. However, they are overlooking the fact that it is not an 'authorised published Grand Lodge ritual'. There isn't one. The first ritual to be published did not appear until 1838. However, the Emulation Lodge of Improvement, the governing body of Emulation ritual did eventually authorise a publication in 1969 – this is our present 'little blue book'.

Although I am here referring to Emulation, as we know there are many other forms, including Taylor's, Metropolitan, Nigerian, Claret, etc. However, the same principle applies.

But do we have to follow it to the letter? The answer is no, we do not. The *Book of Constitutions* Rule 155 states: *'The members present at any Lodge duly summoned have an undoubted right to regulate their own proceedings, provided they are consistent with the general laws and regulations of the Craft.'*

In other words, as long as too many innovations are not introduced, they would be acceptable. So minor amendments to the ritual, the use of words which are slightly different or movements in the ceremonial which one Lodge does differently to another, do not matter.

By having these differences, I think it makes Masonry more interesting, especially when you witness them in another Lodge.

Opening in Which Degree?

Traditionally, English Lodges open into the First Degree and all work is normally carried out in that degree unless there is a Passing ceremony, a Raising ceremony or the Installation of a Master.

In English Lodges, it is customary to open in each degree in turn, First to Second to Third. But we do not always close in full and often the Master will ask the Principal Officers (the two Wardens) to stand and then declare: *'By virtue of the power vested in me as the Master of this Lodge, I close the Lodge in … degree and labour is resumed in the …. degree'.* This is commonly known as 'closing by virtue'.

Often the reverse happens, especially at an Installation when the Lodge opens up to the Third to receive senior officers and then closes by virtue or adjourns and resumes in the Second for the Installation ceremony to commence.

However, some Lodges practise the opening and closing of each degree in turn, in full, at all meetings.

English Lodges are entitled to work three degrees and the Masters' Installation but no more. However, in Scotland they may work the three degrees, including the Mark Degree (done separately) and the Installation, and the Lodges may open directly into the Third Degree when electing officers.

The opening and closing of Lodges in Scotland, in the First, Second and Third Degrees is considerably longer than that in England and includes much of what was lost to English Masonry at the time of the Union.

In Ireland, the three degrees and the Installation of a Master are worked except that the period between degrees is a minimum of three months, whereas in England it is one month and Scotland two weeks.

In Irish Masonry, as with Scottish, there is a more extensive ceremonial than we find in English ritual, particularly the opening where each Brother has to give a password in turn to the Wardens as they go around the Lodge. They may sometimes also open up directly in the Third Degree.

In the USA, it is normal for a Lodge to open directly into the Third Degree and most of the normal work of the Lodge is done in that degree.

There, the First and Second Degrees are used for Initiation and Passing and in most American Lodges an Entered Apprentice and a Fellowcraft are not regarded as members of the Lodge and are therefore not admitted, except for degree purposes.

It is not until you are raised to a Master Mason that you will become a member and receive your 'Dues Card', which records that you have paid your Lodge subscription which allows you to visit another Lodge.

If you get the chance, try visiting another Constitution. However, be prepared to be tested, unless there is a Brother of that particular Constitution able to vouch for you as a Mason.

Pillars

The subject of pillars to a new Mason can be very confusing, as there are several references to them in our ritual. Let us take a closer look to try and remove some of that confusion.

We first find pillars being mentioned in one of the Old Charges, the *Cooke MS* of 1420, in the legendary history of the craft in which two pillars were erected by the children of Lamech to preserve the wisdom of their day. One was made of brick as a protection against fire and the other of marble to protect against flood. However, these now have no place in our modern ritual.

Most of us are familiar with the two great pillars placed at the porch-way or entrance of King Solomon's Temple. These can be found in the Old Testament (I Kings 7:15-22). The one on the left was named B...z and that on the right J....n.

In many of our Lodge rooms they are placed either side of the entrance. In some they are placed behind the Master's chair and in the old Lodge room in Wigan, two massive hollow pillars were placed on the edge of the carpet. These are now in the entrance inside the Lodge room at Bryn Masonic Hall and contain various artefacts, placed in them when they were moved and refurbished.

On top of many pillars can be found the terrestrial and celestial globes. These are also to be found on the Warden's columns. Should they be there? Well, historians believe that when the Geneva Bible appeared - the first Bible with illustrations - what should have been interpreted as bowls on top of the pillars (probably containing oil to light the room in which they stood) were mistaken for globes by our early devisers of the ritual and that is how they have been shown since.

But on our Grand Lodge certificate we have three pillars. These are not the ones from the entrance to King Solomon's Temple, these are the three great pillars, which emblematically support a Freemasons' Lodge: those of Wisdom, Strength and Beauty. That in the centre is of the Ionic order, that on the left of the Doric order and that on the right of the Corinthian order, representing Solomon, King of Israel; Hiram, King of Tyre; and Hiram Abiff.

They are also mentioned in the Lecture on the First Degree Tracing Board, but slightly differently. Wisdom to contrive, Strength to support and Beauty to adorn.

As we know, there are five types of pillars: Ionic, Doric, Corinthian, Tuscan and Composite, representing the Five Orders of Architecture. The Ionic denotes the Master of a Lodge, representing wisdom. The Senior Warden's, the Doric, represents strength, and the Junior Warden's, the Corinthian, represents beauty.

At one time there may have been three smaller pillars drawn on the floor of the Lodge, again representing Wisdom, Strength and Beauty, but we now have Lodge furniture and the three candlesticks have replaced the drawings, resulting in the Master now having only one pillar (the candlestick). However, the Wardens have two, a candlestick and a column of office.

Masonic tradition is indeed a strange thing!

Preparation of The Candidate for Initiation

We as Freemasons have all been prepared for our Initiation and we are all familiar with the physical side of this preparation. But what of the other side, or spiritual element of it?

How many of us have ever heard an explanation of our spiritual preparation? Not many, I suspect. W. L. Wilmshurst in his *Meaning of Masonry* refers to it as preparation for a new beginning: '*Initiation … what does it really mean and intend? It means a new beginning; a breakaway from an old method and order of life and the entrance upon a new one of larger self-knowledge, deepened understanding and intensified virtue...'*

On the continent it is not uncommon for a candidate to be met at the door of the Masonic Hall and immediately blindfolded. He has read to him a sort of contract in which he promises not to disclose what takes place and that he comes of his own free will. The candidate is placed in a room adjoining the Lodge in which there is a table and chair, a candle and a piece of paper and pencil. The blindfold is removed and he is asked to contemplate for a while and then write down his reasons why he wants to become a Freemason. This is completely separate from any ritual he may undertake.

In some Constitutions there are questions written down for him to answer and an hourglass put in front of him. Therefore he has only limited time in which to answer. Of course, the door to the chamber is not locked and he is free to leave at any time.

This exercise is meant to prepare the candidate for the spiritual change which he is about to experience. On a new life, away from the popular world. All of us have placed our trust in someone we did not necessarily know as we were blindfolded and led almost helpless into that strange environment called a Lodge.

For all of us at some point, Freemasonry is new; some of us are happy to attend our Lodge meetings and enjoy the company of good men, some are happy and contented with the social and benevolent ideals and yet others experience something special in Freemasonry, which is beyond the mere words of the ritual.

When you are asked 'What is Freemasonry?' you may respond that it is about charity and caring and that it is sometimes difficult to explain what Freemasonry is. Why? Because it is about the experience and that may be different for all of us. How do you explain that experience?

I will quote Wilmshurst again: *'"Know thyself" was the injunction inscribed over the portals of ancient Temples of Initiation, for with that knowledge was promised the knowledge of all secrets and all mysteries. And Masonry was designed to teach self-knowledge. But self-knowledge involves knowledge much deeper, vaster and more difficult than is popularly conceived. It is not to be acquired by the formal passage through three or four degrees in as many months; it is a knowledge impossible of full achievement until knowledge of every other kind has been laid aside and a difficult path of life, long and strenuously pursued, that alone fits and leads its followers to its attainment.'*

Provincial Officers

Every Lodge in the English Constitution has Provincial or District Officers, but who are they and what is their status? District Officers are those under the English Constitution meeting overseas.

Provincial Officers have not always existed. Prior to the Union of the two Grand Lodges in 1813, only one of the Grand Lodges, the so-called s' had them. The other Grand Lodge, the Antients, did not have Provinces so there was no need for intermediate ranks between Lodge and Grand Lodge. Each of their Lodges reported directly to Grand Lodge, whereas the Moderns had Provincial Grand Lodges to whom their Lodges reported.

The first Provincial Grand Lodge under the Moderns was Cheshire in 1726 and others quickly followed. A Provincial Grand Master is so appointed at the prerogative of the Grand Master himself and he ranks immediately behind the Assistant Grand Master.

In the early days it was not uncommon for a PGM to appoint all of his Provincial Officers from his own Lodge, something which as the number of Lodges grew, became very unpopular.

Today, subordinate Provincial Officers are appointed by the PGM from across the Province. Their ranks, with one or two exceptions, mirror those of

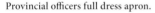
Provincial officers full dress apron.

Masonic pageantry – the procession into Provincial Grand Lodge.

a Lodge - Provincial Senior Grand Wardens being the highest rank and so on. There are two types of Provincial Officers, Acting and Past.

Acting Officers are appointed for one year only, except for the Provincial Grand Treasurer Secretary and Deputy and Assistants, whose appointment is usually for an extended period of time as they are appointed to run the administration of the Province. There are other Acting Officers whose appointment may also be semi-permanent: The Grand Chaplain, Organist, Director of Ceremonies, Mentor, Orator, Tyler and Pursuivant are the usual ones.

Past ranks are generally awarded to Brethren who have occupied the office of Master of a Lodge. They are generally awarded after eight years' service, but for exceptional service this may be less. The ranks are generally the same as a Lodge, except there is a Provincial Grand Superintendent of Works, a rank not held in a Lodge.

Promotion can depend on several things and a former Acting Officer will generally receive promotion earlier than a non-Acting Officer. Although, having said that, this is not *always* the case.

Each Lodge Secretary is expected to keep a record of those who are eligible for appointment to Provincial rank, the offices they have held, and what particular work they have done. External appointments, such as being a JP

Procession out of Provincial Grand Lodge.

and other work for the community, are also taken into account. However, each Province has its own system for awarding 'honours' as it is generally called.

Brethren who are not Past Masters of a Lodge may be considered for 'honours', especially if they have occupied an office in the Lodge. However, their appointment is generally after a good number of years of service.

All Provincial Officers wear dark blue regalia with the badge of office shown on their apron with the name of the Province surrounding it. Provincial Stewards wear red regalia. A Past Master will have levels on his apron whilst those who have not reached the Chair retain the rosettes, but this time in dark blue. District Grand Lodges are similar and have the same ranks as a Province.

Salutations

I have been asked many times, what is the significance of salutations and when did they start? The subject of salutations is a complicated one and the answer is not straightforward.

Salutations in Freemasonry occur at and on different occasions. For example, a visiting Grand Officer in a Provincial Lodge may be saluted shortly after he has entered or later as the case may be and depending on his status it may be three for a Grand Officer or five in the case of a Deputy, Assistant or Past Assistant Provincial Grand Master and seven for the Provincial Grand Master.

What are salutations and when should they be given? Well, after a new Master has been installed it is customary to give five 'Grand or Royal signs' five times during the Inner Workings. At this point it is given audibly, with a clap of the hands.

Also during the ceremony of Installation after the Board of Installed Masters has been closed and the Brethren are re-admitted it is customary to give three MMs signs as a salutation in passing around the Lodge, when the FCs enter to give the H H, Badge salutation five times and finally when EAs enter to give the EA sign three times. However, Emulation is the only ritual that requires that the signs given at this time should be audible.

What is the significance of the numbers? The answer is 'none'. According to the late Harry Carr the question of salutes was discussed by eminent members of QC in 1916 when it was generally agreed that 'three-five-three' is the correct procedure in Lodge at an Installation. This may be because at the Consecration of a new Lodge the guidance is the salutes should be three-five-three. He goes on to say that at some unknown point they probably had some Masonic significance being related to other numbered items in ritual practice, e.g. three steps in the First Degree, five in the Second and seven in the Third. However, seven was dropped because seven is reserved for a Provincial or District Grand Master.

It is generally agreed that when the Grand or Royal sign is used as a salutation it should be silent, without a clap of hands, or audible slap against the body except as stated previously.

Rituals other than Emulation vary in their requirements: Claret is five-five-three and Humber is three Grand or Royal signs for the MM, five Ht, Apr, Hd for FCs and only one EA sign for the Apprentices.

Grand Honours were not approved until 1930 as an amendment to the 1926 *B of C* and the number of salutes three, five, seven, nine and eleven has no significance other than to distinguish rank, nine being reserved for the Deputy Grand Master and Assistant and finally eleven reserved for the Grand and Pro Grand Master.

'Salutations or honours' given at a Festive Board are not laid down and differ widely from province to province and are dependent to a large degree on the custom and practice of each Lodge. Most are short and to the point whilst others are quite lengthy and require the use of various hand movements which are too varied to describe in a short paper such as this.

Finally, the list of prefixes to Grand Rank and the number of salutes are given in the *Book of Constitutions* at Rule 6. The protocol for who receives what and when is extremely complicated and depends on the occasion, and is explained clearly in Graham Redman's book *Masonic Etiquette Today* which I would recommend everyone to read.

Secretary and Treasurer

In an English Lodge, the 'regular' officers are a Master, two Wardens, a Treasurer, Secretary, two Deacons, an Inner Guard and a Tyler. But this was not always the case.

All of the early Lodges had a Secretary, but not always a Treasurer. Sometimes the roles would be combined where the Secretary also did the job of Treasurer. Before 1813 and the Union of the two Grand Lodges, the Secretary was senior to the Treasurer (where there was one), and then it changed to its present form.

Nowadays, the Treasurer is given precedence immediately before the Secretary, but whereas the Secretary may be appointed by the Worshipful Master, the Treasurer must be elected by ballot in open Lodge, unless there are no other nominations and the Brethren have been notified of this on the summons convening the meeting, then he may be 'declared' as Treasurer unopposed.

The Treasurer's responsibility is to look after the financial affairs of the Lodge, to collect subscriptions and to ensure that Lodge accounts are paid and the annual dues are paid to Grand and Provincial Lodge. His insignia of office is a key.

The Secretary, on the other hand, looks after the administrative affairs of the Lodge. He deals with correspondence with Grand Lodge, Provincial Grand Lodge, (Group or District in larger Provinces) and other general correspondence. He is responsible for issuing the summons, convening the Lodge in good time, either by post or as is more frequent nowadays by e-mail. He is generally the first point of contact for a Lodge and the role is a key office. A good Secretary can help to make a Lodge run smoothly, whereas an inefficient one can cause a Lodge to lose its way and become discontented and dysfunctional.

In many Lodges, it is the Secretary's responsibility to arrange the catering for the Lodge at festive boards and to accept apologies from Brethren who cannot attend a meeting.

One of the chief tools of a good Secretary is a 'crystal ball' which he will use on a regular basis to try and figure out what is going on in the minds of the members of the Lodge, particularly in relation to the intentions of individual Brethren, who sometimes do not advise him if they are attending a meeting or staying for a meal. A powerful crystal ball is an asset to a Secretary.

Brethren, I am sure you will appreciate that having to use a crystal ball in these days of advanced technology is a bit old-fashioned and you can help considerably to lessen its use by keeping the Secretary informed of what you intend to do in good time. Good manners cost nothing!

The badge of office of a Secretary is 'two crossed pens in saltire', two crossed feathered quills reminding us of the time when the inkwell and quill pen were commonly used by the holder of the office.

So Mote It Be

How familiar that phrase is. No Lodge is ever opened or closed, in due form, without using it. Yet few know how old it is, much less what a deep meaning it carries. Like so many old things, it is so near to us that we do not hear it.

As far back as we can go in the annals of the Craft we find this old phrase. Its form betrays its age. The word 'mote' is an Anglo-Saxon word, derived from an anomalous verb, 'motan'. Chaucer uses the exact phrase in the same sense in which we use it, meaning: *'So May It Be.'* It is found in the Regius Poem of 1390, the oldest document of the Craft, just as we use it today.

In it are the words: '...*after a closing prayer adds: 'Amen, amen, so mote it be, say so all, for charity'*. And in the *Cooke MS* of 1410: *'Amen, so mote it be.'*

So, we hear it in the Lodge at opening, at closing, and at the hour of Initiation. No Mason ever enters upon any great or important undertaking without invoking the aid of Deity. And he ends his prayer with the old phrase: *'So Mote It Be.'*

Harry Carr in his book *The Freemason at Work* describes it as:

> *'The phrase literally means 'So be it' and it was used in the Middle Ages in England as a pious finale to prayers or blessings. It should be noted that the medieval formula began with the Hebrew word 'Amen' which has fallen out of Masonic usage. The word 'Amen' has a range of meanings all related to fidelity, constancy, sureness and trust, and when used at the end of Hebrew prayers and blessings, it was a formula of acquiescence and confirmation, as though to say 'Truly we believe that it is (or will) be so.'*

Thus although the *'Amen'* and *'So Mote It Be'* do not have the same original meaning, they have virtually acquired the same meaning in the course of centuries, and this possibly explains the modern omission of the *'Amen'* in Masonic usage.

Some believe that the response to 'grace' at the Festive Board should be 'Amen', especially when there may be ladies or non-Masons present, leaving 'So Mote It Be' for use only in Lodge.

That's one for us to think about.

Some Lost Symbols of English Craft Masonry

At the time of the Union of the two Grand Lodges in 1813, many ancient Masonic symbols fell into disuse and unless you happen to come across an old floor-cloth or an engraving in a book, you are unlikely to encounter them in today's Freemasonry and certainly not in the Craft, except perhaps in Bristol or in certain 'side' degrees.

What were these symbols? Well, here are just some of them with a brief explanation for each; all are symbolic of the Master Mason's Degree.

Read carefully the words in each:

The Beehive: 'The Beehive is an emblem of industry and recommends the practice of that virtue to all created beings, from the highest seraph in heaven, to the lowest reptile of the dust. It teaches us, that as we came into this world, rational and intelligent beings, so we should ever be industrious ones, never sitting down contented while our fellow-creatures around us are in want, when it is our power to relieve them, without inconvenience to ourselves.'

The Pot of Incense: 'Is an emblem of a pure heart, which is always an acceptable sacrifice to the Deity, and, as this glows with fervent heat, so should the Freemason's heart continually glow with gratitude to the great beneficent Author of our existence, for the manifold blessings we enjoy.'

The Anchor and the Ark: 'Are emblems of a well-grounded hope, and a well-spent life. They are emblematical of that Divine Ark which safely carries us over this tempestuous sea of troubles, and that Anchor which shall safely moor us in a peaceful harbour, where the wicked shall cease from troubling and the weary shall find rest.'

The Hourglass: 'Is an emblem of human life. Behold! How swiftly the sands run and how rapidly our lives are drawing to a close! We cannot without astonishment behold the little particles which are contained in the machine - how they pass away almost imperceptibly! And yet, to our surprise, in the space of a short hour, they are all exhausted. Thus wastes man! Today, he puts forth the tender leaves of hope, tomorrow blossoms, and bears his blushing honours thick upon him; the next day comes a frost, which nips the shoot; and when he thinks his greatness is still aspiring, he falls like autumn leaves to enrich our mother earth.'

The Scythe: 'The scythe is an emblem of time, which cuts the brittle thread of life, and launches us into eternity. Behold! What havoc the scythe of time makes among the human race! If by chance we should escape the numerous evils incident to childhood and youth, and with health and vigour arrive to the years of manhood; yet withal we must soon be cut down by that all-devouring scythe of time, and be gathered into the land where our fathers have gone before us.'

The Trowel: 'The working tools of a Freemason are all the implements of Masonry indiscriminately; but more especially the trowel. The trowel is an instrument made use of by operative masons, to spread the cement which unites a building into one common mass; but we, as free and accepted and speculative Masons, are taught to make use of it for the more noble and glorious purpose of spreading brotherly love and affection; that cement which unites us into one sacred band, or society of friends and brothers, among whom no contention should ever exist, but that noble contention, or rather emulation, of who can best work and best agree.'

Take heed of these wonderful words, Brethren.

Squaring the Lodge

Why do we square the Lodge? A question which has been asked many times. How did it arise?

It seems that in the early days of Freemasonry, when the Craft became rather more organised and met in taverns or hostelries, a Lodge would use a room, more than likely upstairs, which had to be prepared for every meeting.

The Lodge furnishings, candlesticks, candles, possibly minute books, symbols such as squares and compasses and working tools would be kept under lock and key in a large wooden trunk known as an 'ark'. We have evidence of this from one of the oldest Lodges in Wigan, The Lodge of Sincerity No. 386, the forerunner of the Grand Lodge in Wigan and now Sincerity Lodge No. 3677.

The floors would be made of wood and before each meeting it was the Tyler's responsibility to draw designs on the floor of the Lodge usually in chalk or crayon. After the meeting the youngest Entered Apprentice would clean the floor. The designs drawn on the floor preceded tracing cloths or Tracing Boards and of course when the members of a Lodge were perambulating around what were quite likely small rooms they had to avoid standing on the chalk designs to as not to obliterate them. It is possibly from this that we have the habit of 'squaring the Lodge'.

However, Dr. E. H. Cartwright, in his book *A Commentary on the Freemasonic Ritual* suggests that everyone passing around the room or moving about should 'square the Lodge' that is, should follow the periphery of a rectangle, the sides of which just clear the pedestals, and that this is following the squares, levels and perpendicular principle. However, he deplores the practice of halting at each corner and making play with one's feet like a sentry turning, which introduces an undesirable element of comedy into the proceedings.

There is also a mention of perambulations around a floor-cloth in '*Reception d'un Frey-Macon*', from 1737 which says that the candidate was '*…made to take three tours in the Chamber, around a space marked on the floor, where…at the two sides of this space they have also drawn in crayon a great J and a great B*'.

Harry Carr in *The Freemason at Work* says: '*Most workings nowadays square the Lodge, clockwise, during the ceremonies, but exaggerated squaring, which requires all movements to be made clockwise round the floor of the Lodge and forbids crossing diagonally during ordinary business, probably arose in the mid-1800s. The word "exaggerated" is used deliberately here, because the practice is often carried to extremes which are a waste of valuable time…*'

Please note, Brethren, 'squaring' does not apply in other Orders in Freemasonry.

Stewards

The dictionary definition of a Steward is: '*A person who manages the domestic concerns of a family or institution…someone who helps with arrangements.*'

The old English guilds had their Stewards and no doubt Freemasonry

District Steward's Apron, Madras.

District Grand Steward's collar and gauntlets, Madras.

inherited them from that source. Moderns Lodges had Stewards who did work which in the Ancients Lodges was done by the Deacons. The Steward is one of the 'additional' officers who may be appointed by the Worshipful Master of a Lodge.

Prior to the Union, Stewards occupied a more senior place in Moderns Lodges, ranking just after the Secretary, and they even outranked the Deacons where a Lodge had them. However, this was lost at the Union and nowadays they rank above the Tyler and before the Inner Guard. The office of Steward is often the first rung of the ladder in a Lodge and gives the new Mason the chance to show what he can do. A good Steward will learn the duties of the next couple of offices above his and may be called upon to occupy those positions if required.

Not too long ago Stewards waited on the tables at Festive Boards, providing drinks to those Brethren who required them, and this practice still exists in some Lodges even today.

There are three other Stewards in Freemasonry: the Charity Steward, which is an office which was only introduced in 1975 (this office is the subject of a separate paper), and then there are Provincial or District Grand Stewards and Grand Stewards.

The latter are appointed by the Grand Master from nineteen specified London Lodges who have the right to nominate a Grand Steward. To be a Grand Steward is a great honour and it can be an expensive one as well, as the appointed Grand Stewards originally paid for the whole of the Grand Festival banquet held annually. They were allowed to charge a nominal dining fee but they had to cover any shortfall.

Even today it may be an expensive office to hold. Their regalia is red instead of Garter blue. The Grand Stewards Lodge is the first on the Roll of Lodges under UGL and ranks without number before the Grand Masters Lodge No.1.

The other Stewards are the Provincial and District Grand Stewards who also wear red regalia and are often seen accompanying senior officers with their white wands on special occasions (see The Masonic Apron).

They are not responsible financially for any festivities in their Province or District, but they too have their own Lodge and only Past Stewards are eligible to become members.

The jewel of the Steward is the Cornucopia or 'Horn of Plenty'.

Tenets and Principles

A 'tenet' is described in the *Oxford English Dictionary* as: *'a doctrine, dogma, principle, or opinion in religion, philosophy, politics or the like, held by a school, sect, party or person'* and 'principle' as: *'a primary element, force, or law, which produces or determines particular results; the ultimate basis upon which the existence of something depends; cause, in the widest sense.'*

The *Book of Constitutions* of the United Grand Lodge of England frequently refers to *'Principles'* but does not mention 'tenets'; they are referred to only in our ritual.

According to *Chambers Dictionary*, 'tenets' are *'any opinion, principle or doctrine which a person holds or maintains as true'*. An example of this could be the belief in the immortality of the soul. The definition of 'principle' given in *Chambers* is: *'a source, root, origin; a fundamental or primary cause, a beginning etc.'*

The Aims and Relationships in the *Book of Constitutions* states at No. 2: *'In view of the representations which have been received, and of statements recently issued which have distorted or obscured the true objects of Freemasonry, it is once again considered necessary to emphasize certain fundamental principles of the Order'*. It then continues to outline the aims and relationships of the Craft followed by the Basic Principles for Grand Lodge Recognition, concluding at No. 8 with: *'the principles of the Antient Landmarks, customs and usages of the Craft shall be strictly observed'*.

Take a look at them, Brethren, and you will see why principles are so important.

Finally may I quote from Harry Carr:

> *'Tenets are beliefs that we hold, even though they are beyond proof. They may be our own invention, or inherited, but we do not question them because they are founded in our faith.*
>
> *'Principles may have their roots in natural law, or in ethics and philosophies which shape our conduct. But they may also be*

invented or adopted rules or beliefs, which have their basic force as 'principle' simply because we choose to acknowledge them as such.'

The 47th Problem of Euclid

In the English Constitution, a Past Master of a Lodge wears a light blue collar with a silver stripe down the centre. His badge is the Square with the 47th Problem of Euclid within a quadrant suspended from the point of the collar.

The 47th Problem of Euclid or the Pythagorean Theorem is the famous theorem about right angles: namely that the sum of the squares of the legs is equal to the square of the hypotenuse: $A^2 + B^2 = C^2$.

In old ritual it was described as:

> *'The 47th Problem of Euclid was an invention of our ancient friend and Brother, the great Pythagoras. This wise philosopher enriched his mind abundantly with a general knowledge of things, and more especially geometry or masonry. On this subject he drew up many problems and theorems and amongst the most distinguished, he erected this, which in the joy of his heart, he call Eureka (in the Grecian language, "I have found it"). It teaches masons to be general lovers of the arts and sciences.'*

Firstly, it was not Pythagoras who discovered the rule that is referenced by his name. The Egyptians used this principle long before Pythagoras set it down to measure their fields after the annual Nile floods had washed away the boundary markers. Pythagoras is the man who *proved* that the process works.

In the USA, which follows many of the old Masonic traditions, a Past Master's jewel is generally the Compasses upon a sector of a circle with the Sun in the centre, except in Pennsylvania where it is the same as in England.

The Compasses with the Sun in the centre on a sector of a circle is now of course the jewel of the Grand Master and Pro Grand Master of the United Grand Lodge of England.

Why was the 47th proposition chosen? Harry Carr suggests that: *'Geometry, in the design of buildings and in the practice of the mason trade, had always been closely linked with the Craft. Indeed the Old Charges constantly re-iterate the link between Geometry and Masonry, even to the extent of outright declaration that "Geometry is now called Masonr"'…'*

When Dr. Anderson, in his 1723 *Constitutions* averred that: '*…the 47th Proposition of Euclid's first book …is the foundation of all Masonry, sacred,* *civil and military*', he was treating the 47th proposition as the symbol of all Geometry, and proclaimed the age-old link between that science and the Craft.

Anderson also showed it on the front of his *Constitutions* in 1723 and 1738, and is the *quintessence of perfection and truth.*

The Ashlars

In most English Masonic Lodges there are two Ashlars, the Rough and Perfect Ashlars, which are regarded along with the Tracing Boards as the immovable jewels of a Lodge.

An Ashlar is prepared or 'dressed' stonework of any type of stone used in masonry. It is used to describe the hewn or dressed stone which comes from the quarries, to distinguish it from the rough or un-hewn stone.

The Ashlars used in Freemasonry are part of the 'furniture' of the Lodge and in many the Rough Ashlar is situated at the North corner and the Smooth or Perfect Ashlar at South-East corner of the floor of the Lodge. Also in some Lodges a Perfect Ashlar is suspended by a 'Lewis' from a tripod.

However, it is not uncommon to find them in front of the Senior and Junior Wardens on the floor in front of pedestals or even as miniatures on the pedestals themselves.

Symbolically, the Rough Ashlar represents the uninitiated Mason as he enters into his journey through Freemasonry, whilst the Smooth Ashlar represents the mature Mason who has passed through his Masonic education and has worked according to the line and rule and constantly strives to achieve enlightenment. J. P. Lomas states: *'It is also a perfect cube with each side equal, symbolising that a Freemason should present the same side to the world at large at all times.'*

Historically, they have been around a long time and are referred to in Prichard's exposure, *Masonry Dissected*, of 1730 where the Rough Ashlar (but not the smooth) is mentioned as one of the three immovable jewels. They are also mentioned in early French Masonic exposures.

In the *Freemasons' Guide and Compendium* Bernard Jones mentions that: *'In 1655, in his Commentary, William Gouge, D.D. wrote; "Unless we be quickned and made living stones fit for a spiritual building; unless we be gathered together and united to Christ the foundation, and one to another, as mutual parts of the same building, we can never make up a Temple for God to dwell in."*

He also tells us that: *'an Ashlar is any wall building stone whose main angles are right angles; however, the speculatives' Ashlar is a cubical stone, although the 'perfect' Ashlar originally was probably not cubical but a perpend stone by which name it was known to our early Brethren…'* A true perpend goes through the wall and is oblong with both end faces exposed.

In some Lodges their Ashlars are of the perpend shape, not cubes.

Take a look next time you visit another Lodge.

The Candidate

All of us have experienced the night when we came along to the Lodge to be initiated as a Mason, somewhat bewildered and perhaps a bit worried; what in some ways was a traumatic but enlightening experience.

The bewilderment is heightened when the Tyler tells us what is needed before our entry into the Lodge. Do this and that, roll up your trouser leg, (why did they ask me to come in a suit?). No metal. What is it all for?

Well may you ask - but the explanation is simple. It is historical. For centuries mankind has undergone initiatory rites and although ours is relatively new, just a few hundred years old, what we are doing is following something which humans have certainly done since Roman times - and possibly before.

The word 'candidate' comes from the Latin word *'candidatus'*, meaning 'clothed in white' - as Roman candidates for office were required to wear the white robe, the *'toga candida'*. Also, the word 'initiate' is derived from the Latin *'initium'*, 'beginning'.

He is also sl…..d. This again bears the character of antiquity. In ancient tradition it was a gesture of reverence, as it was not considered proper to enter a temple unless the feet were bare. Symbolically, the candidate is entering on consecrated ground.

In some old English Lodges and on the continent, it is not uncommon for a candidate to have to strip down to his underclothes and put on a white suit, torn in various parts and perhaps cut off at the knees. This is to signify that the candidate is in a state of distress, poor and without means, and of course no matter what his state, he is ignorant of what is to come. He may also be placed in a bare room with nothing but a table, chair and a candle to light the room. He may be given a piece of paper and a pencil and asked to write down why he wishes to become a Mason. He is then left alone to contemplate. Of course, he is free to walk away at any time.

Eventually, as he waits outside the door of the Lodge, many things pass through his mind. The Tyler takes hold of him and from then on he places his trust in those who are to lead him into the Lodge room.

He can hear, but he cannot see, he can feel and he is able to answer the questions put to him. He is able to walk with a Deacon holding him as a guide.

All of this symbolism represents that a man comes into Freemasonry in a complete state of submission and with an open mind. He is asked: *'In whom do you put your trust?'* He replies: *'In God'*, indicating to him that no harm will come to him if he is true to God, himself and his fellow man. He discovers that he is not entering easily or lightly into our Order and he will also discover that trust will play a big part in his life as a Freemason.

He has already made a declaration that he is a free man, of 21 years of age and comes of his own free will and accord. Now in a part of the ceremony he is expected to take an obligation with his hands upon the Volume of the Sacred Law, an obligation which he will remember for the rest of his life.

His special journey has begun.

The Chequered Pavement

It has been suggested that the floor of King Solomon's Temple was adorned with a chequered design; however, there is no evidence to confirm this.

The black and white chequered carpet design did not appear in our Lodge rooms until the end of the 18th century. Prior to that a design would be drawn in chalk or charcoal on the floor of the room of the hostelry in which the Lodge meeting was being held.

These were the forerunners of our present-day Tracing Boards and would show various symbols including squares, levels and plumb-rules, a point within a circle embordered by two parallel lines, compasses and other designs. These would be removed after every meeting, either by the Tyler or the youngest Entered Apprentice in the Lodge.

The drawings were later replaced by floor-cloths, several of which are still in existence. Of course these would be rolled up after each meeting and placed in the 'Ark' or box belonging to the Lodge.

We do not know the precise date when the chequered carpet or mosaic pavement began to appear, but we do know that it was common in ancient buildings, even as far back as Roman times, to have such a design and the Masons adopted it for their Lodges.

J. S. M. Ward wrote of the carpet or flooring: *'The Inner meaning of this carpet is the chequered way of life – the alternations of joy and sorrow, of good and evil, of day and night, which we all experience in the course of our lives.'* He went on to say: *'But what probably strikes the initiate more than anything else about this carpet are the four tassels which are woven into the pattern at the four corners. We are told that these represent the four cardinal virtues.'* These are of course Prudence, Temperance, Fortitude and Justice.

When we 'square' the Lodge, we are continuing an old tradition from when the drawings on the floor in the room in a hostelry were done in chalk and charcoal. To step on them could erase the design which had been carefully prepared for the meeting - and woe betide anyone who did. He would be admonished by the Master and probably fined as well. Nowadays, of course, we try most of the time to avoid stepping on the pavement, particularly in the Craft. In other degrees it is not so important and squaring does not take place.

In many Constitutions, the Mosaic pavement is not used, particularly in America, and carpets may be blue, in some cases red, or the floor may be just plain wood.

It is like many things in Freemasonry - we have attached symbolism to it to suit our needs.

The Deacons

The Moderns Grand Lodge of 1717 did not have Deacons until about 1809. Lodges working under their jurisdiction would have had Stewards carrying out the role we now know as Deacon.

Having said that, I am now about to contradict myself - because some Moderns Lodges *did* use Deacons, even though their Grand Lodge frowned upon them. Those Lodges were probably influenced by the Antients Grand Lodge. The Lodges had Deacons shortly after its formation from 1751. This Grand Lodge had a great deal of Irish influence - Deacons in Ireland were regarded as a very important office and Lodges there had them as early as 1727.

The term 'Deacon' was used in churches in James I's time; however, the Masonic term comes to us through Scotland where it was not unknown for the chief officer of a Lodge to be known as the Deacon, with Wardens assisting him.

The original Masonic role of a Deacon was a 'messenger' or an assistant for the Master and Wardens of a Lodge and he would carry messages from one to the other.

This is carried over into our modern ritual, when at the opening of a Lodge the Master first asks the Junior Deacon his place and his duty, which is '*To carry all messages and communications of the Worshipful Master from the Senior to the Junior Warden and see that the same are punctually obeyed*' and the Senior Deacon says: '*To bear all messages and commands from the WM to the SW and await the return of the JD*' (Emulation).

Formerly, messages would be whispered between the WM, the Wardens and Deacons as can be seen by this extract from the ritual of Calling Off and Calling On as revealed in the exposure of 1760 '*Three Distinct Knocks*': '*The*

Master whispers to the Senior deacon at his right, and says: ''tis my will and pleasure that this Lodge is called off from work to refreshment during pleasure. Then the Senior Deacon carries it to the Senior Warden and whispers the same words in his ear…etc.'

This practice has now ceased and, in fact, apart from obtaining the signatures of the Master and the two wardens for the minutes, and/or attending to the Tracing Boards and perhaps the collection plates, they no longer act as messengers. However, they do play a very important part during the ceremonies of Initiation, Passing and Raising.

The modern Deacons carry wands which are ancient emblems of office but again I refer to the exposure *'Three Distinct Knocks': 'The Master and the two Deacons have a black rod in their hands about 7 foot high, when they open the Lodge and close it.'* The wands today are no longer black and much less than seven feet long.

The emblem of a Deacon's wand is a Dove with an Olive Branch, believed to symbolise the messenger sent from the Ark by Noah. Since the founding of United Grand Lodge, it has replaced the figure of Mercury with winged feet and helmet.

However, the latter has been retained by Deacons in the Mark Degree and by some very old Craft Lodges, especially in the North of England.

The Director of Ceremonies

A Director of Ceremonies in a Lodge is one of the 'additional' officers along with a Chaplain and Assistant DC, Almoner, Organist, Assistant Secretary and Stewards.

There is one other 'additional' office which did not come into use until 1975, that of Charity Steward.

The office of Director of Ceremonies only came into being from 1884 when the *Book of Constitutions* stated: *'The Master may also appoint a Chaplain, a Director of Ceremonies, an Organist and Stewards...'*

The jewel of his office is two rods in saltire, tied by a ribbon, and his duties are to guide the Lodge during its ceremonial. It is a very important office and one which can either enhance the reputation of a Lodge or demean it. In most Lodges the Director of Ceremonies carries a wand which is the emblem of his office, but there are a few where he will carry a short baton instead.

A 'good DC', as he is commonly known, is a linchpin in the workings of a Lodge and it is from him that all other 'floor' officers will seek guidance. He will assist the Master with the workings of the Lodge according to the requirements of a particular meeting and he is there to assist the Master with the good ruling and governing of a Lodge. His is a very important office and one to which many Brethren aspire; however, few achieve the high standard required to be a 'good DC'.

It is his responsibility to organise the processions into and out of the Lodge at opening and closing and he is also responsible in ensuring that the appropriate salutes are given to senior officers when they are present. As a general rule and unless otherwise agreed, he will prompt the various officers of a Lodge during the ceremonials.

In most Lodges there is an Assistant Director of Ceremonies who is there to assist him and in many cases there to 'learn the ropes' with a view to some day taking over the office of DC. He also carries a wand with the same emblem but with the word 'Assistant' superimposed on the crossed wands.

The DC in many Lodges is responsible for the smooth running of the Festive Board and will call the Brethren to order when wine-takings or toasts are to be given.

There are other Directors of Ceremonies: the Provincial Director of Ceremonies is assisted by Deputy Directors who are responsible for the ceremonial related to Provincial Grand Lodge meetings and also when a Senior Provincial Officer is visiting a private Lodge on official business. He will then take responsibility for the ceremonial associated with the visiting Provincial Officer, usually an Assistant Provincial Grand Master and above.

In Grand Lodge, there is the Grand Director of Ceremonies with several Deputies who are responsible for the running of the ceremonial associated with the Grand Lodge meetings or when Senior Grand Officers are visiting away from Grand Lodge.

Generally speaking, when a Lodge has a good meeting and everything goes well it is the DC who will take the credit. However, if it goes badly it is usually the ADC's fault!

The Four Cardinal Virtues

The four cardinal virtues are Temperance, Fortitude, Prudence and Justice and these can be found in the Lectures of the Three Degree of Freemasonry in the sixth section of the First Lecture.

They are also part of the Charge to the Initiate after his Initiation and are also extolled in the Lecture on the First Degree Tracing Board: '*Let prudence direct you, temperance chasten you, fortitude sustain you and let justice be the guide to all your actions.*' Very important words which should stick in the mind of every Mason.

However, they are not new and can be traced back to St. Thomas Aquinas

(1225-74) who defined virtue as 'a good habit of mind by which one lives rightly'. but the concept of 'virtues' can be traced all the way back to Plato in the fourth century BC.

Bernard Jones, referring to symbolism in Early Religious Teaching, quotes a book written by Durandus (a Bishop who died in 1296): *'There is much symbolism on the Masonic pattern.'* Durandus refers in the following quotation (in part):

> *'In the Temple of God the foundation is Faith, which is conversant with unseen things;*
> *the roof is charity, which covereth a multitude of sins. The door is obedience…*
> *'The pavement is humility…*
> *'The four sides, walls, are the four cardinal virtues – justice, fortitude, temperance, prudence.*
> *'Hence the Apocalypse saith, "The city lieth four-square".'*

It has been said that the four tassles at the corners of the mosaic floor carpet refer to the four cardinal virtues and they have also occasionally been depicted on Tracing Boards. Julian Rees refers to them in his book *Tracing Boards of the Three Degrees in Craft Masonry Explained* and in particular to a First Degree Tracing Board belonging to Phoenix Lodge No. 94 where they are depicted by their initials.

Bro. David McReady in his paper given to the Manchester Lodge for Masonic Research *'Some Thoughts on the Cardinal Virtues'* says of Prudence: *'Now strictly speaking, prudence is not a moral value, but an intellectual one because it concerns our actions…'*

Of Temperance he says: *'St Thomas Aquinas …temperance was chiefly concerned with the sense of touch, a sense whose over stimulation he saw as being animalistic, unbecoming of rational creatures...'*

Of Fortitude (courage) he again quotes Aquinas: *'Whosoever stands firm against the greatest of evils will also stand firm against the lesser ones...'* He also distinguishes between two types of courage: *'The first is active, those who go forward in battle…the second is passive, that of martyrs or those who endure in the face of illness or hardship or other suffering show forth the greatest nobility of spirit...'*

And, finally, of Justice: it is the virtue which gives to others what is their due: *'The many precepts which this virtue embraces can be resumed in one basic law…Good is to be done to others, evil towards them avoid, is the law which ought indeed to be the guide to all our actions.'*

The Immediate Past Master

The Immediate Past Master of a Lodge usually sits to the left of the Worshipful Master and will normally have completed his year in office, after installing his successor.

Strictly speaking, he is not an officer of the Lodge but the most junior Past Master. After he has completed a further year as IPM he is simply a Past Master of the Lodge.

His role is to support and assist the current Master to carry out his duties and to deputise for him if he is absent, although the latter duty may be carried out by any Past Master of the Lodge. At the festive board he generally gives a toast to the Master. Under the English Constitution, a Past Master who is a subscribing member of a Lodge is automatically a member of Grand Lodge.

His regalia is light blue, with levels instead of rosettes, and he wears a light blue collar with a central silver stripe. His badge is the square with the 47th Problem of Euclid suspended therefrom.

In other Constitutions such as the Irish and Scottish, things are different. In Ireland, for instance, a Past Master is entitled to a Past Master's Certificate and his name may be entered on the Past Master's Register which is made available at every meeting of the Grand Lodge of Ireland.

In Scotland, the situation of a Past Master is a complicated one, as the Scottish Constitution omits a Past Master from the list of those eligible to become members of Grand Lodge. However, there are other criteria in which a Past Master may be eligible to Grand Lodge membership provided he is in good standing. These are too numerous to mention in a short paper.

In America, there is a degree called the Past Master degree which with that of Mark Master, which it follows, and that of Most Excellent Master, which it precedes, is a forerunner to the Royal Arch. This does not entitle a Brother to the status of a Past Master in the Craft.

A Board of Installed Masters is formed for one purpose and one purpose only and that is to install a Master Elect into the Chair of a Craft Lodge, and only those who have been previously installed as Masters may be present. The ceremony of Installing a Master was not finalised until 1827.

Prior to the Union under the two Grand Lodges, the Moderns did not have an Installation ceremony as such; however, the Antients appear to have had an Installation ceremony at which only Past Masters could be present.

According to Bernard Jones in his book *Freemasons Guide and Compendium*: '*While the ceremonial method of installing a Master does not appear therefore to be more than about two hundred years old, the Charge to the Master includes material going back much earlier...Early speculative masons spoke more of chairing the Master than of installing him. The Installing Master often being called the Chairing Master.'*

The Inner Guard

The introduction of the Inner Guard as an officer of a Lodge is relatively recent and it is only from the late eighteenth century we hear of an Inner Guard.

The role of the Inner Guard was often taken by the youngest Entered Apprentice present and he was known as the door-keeper, was armed with a trowel and was there as an assistant to the Tyler.

Initially, he was known as the Inner Tyler or Inner Guarder and the office was only officially recognised in 1814 after the Union of the two Grand Lodges. It was not until 1819 that United Grand Lodge authorised the jewel of the Inner Guard as two crossed swords. Prior to that, it had been a pointed trowel which is now, of course, the jewel of the Charity Steward.

There is a record in an old Dorset Lodge, the Lodge of Honour & Friendship at Blandford (which ceased to exist in 1838), where a particular Brother was allowed one shilling for each Lodge night and one shilling for every newly initiated brother to take on himself the office of Inner Guard to assist the Tyler. Royal Augustus Lodge in Monmouth, before it ceased to work in 1830, had an Outer Tyler and a Junior Tyler. The Inner Guard is now an unpaid office, but in some places a full-time Tyler is a paid office.

In Scotland and Ireland, the Inner Guard has his place in their Lodges, but in America it is practically unknown. The office is taken by that of the Junior Deacon, acting under the command of the Junior Warden where he assists the Tyler to examine each and every visitor who cannot be vouched for. This is known in America as the 'Tyler's Oath'. The visitor is taken into a side room and is examined, and before the examining officers he repeats the oath that he has been regularly initiated, passed and raised in a just and legally constituted Lodge; that he does not stand suspended or expelled; and knows of no reason why he should not hold Masonic communication with the Brethren. I have personally experienced this type of examination when visiting a Lodge in New York.

The Inner Guard has an important role to play in a Lodge. He must ensure when candidates are being admitted during the ceremonies of Initiation, Passing to the Second Degree and Raising to the Third, that they are correctly prepared accordingly, as required by the ritual, and that they are in possession of the appropriate passwords before he reports to the Junior Warden. He also announces and admits visitors to the Lodge and gives the appropriate knocks on the door of the Lodge according to the degree being worked.

In some Lodges, at the opening and closing, the Inner Guard and the Tyler are part of the procession into the Lodge. At the opening they will report aloud to the Master their respective stations and their duties before taking up post. At the closing they are called in and do likewise.

The Inner Guard is really the first office on the progressive ladder through the Lodge after that of Steward.

The Letter 'G'

As we look around the Lodge room we are likely to see a large letter 'G', sometimes hanging from the ceiling, sometimes located on the floor of the Lodge in the centre or even above and behind the Master's chair. But what is its significance?

Does it mean 'God' or does it stand for 'Geometry'? This debate has gone on for some considerable time. However, when we consider that Freemasonry in England was formerly Christian in nature I would suggest that it stands for

A Lodge-room showing the chequered carpet and the letter 'G' hanging from the ceiling.

the word 'God', for the abbreviation 'G' in ancient times only stood for one thing - God.

It is mentioned in the explanation of the Second Degree Tracing Board and also in the Second Lecture, fifth section of the Lectures of the Three Degrees in Craft Masonry, we find the words:

'Q. When our ancient Brethren were in the middle chamber of the Temple, to what was their attention particularly drawn?
A. Certain Hebrew characters, which are now depicted in a FC's Lodge by the letter 'G'.
Q. What does that letter G denote?
A. GOD the Grand Geometrician of the Universe, to whom we must all submit and whom we ought to adore.'

So both are mentioned but Prichard in his *Masonry Dissected* dated 1730, states:

'Q. Why were you made a fellowcraft?
A. For the sake of the letter 'G.
Q. What does 'G' denote?
A. Geometry the fifth science.'

Masonic scholars have been debating this for centuries. Personally I do not think we will arrive at a definitive answer, although Colin Dyer in his book *Symbolism in Craft Freemasonry* states: '*It is possible that the use of the letter in this way as a representation of God is a reflection of the influence of Jewish tradition in Masonic development. Jewish custom was not to pronounce the name of God which was represented by the tetragrammaton, the four letter JHVH, but to use some other word, such as Adonai (Lord) instead...*'

Which way should it be viewed? From the East or from the West? In most English Lodges it is viewed from the West, especially when it is hanging from the ceiling, but there are many other Lodges, particularly American Lodges, where it is situated behind the Master's chair, so it can only be viewed from the West. In one Lancashire Lodge there is a 'G' hanging from the ceiling when viewed from the West and another placed in the centre of the chequered carpet covered by a white linen cloth. The cloth is only removed when the Lodge is opened in the Second Degree.

Finally, it would seem that the letter 'G' did not make an appearance in Lodges until the mid-eighteenth century and then it was probably drawn on the floor of the Lodge along with other symbols.

The Lodge

The word Lodge derives from the French *'loge'* and was a structure probably made of wood with a thatched roof attached to the side of a building under construction in which stonemasons would work, eat and sleep. We know this because there are many records from various major building projects such as Caernarfon Castle, York Minster and other places which mention the Lodge as a place where masons would take their midday meal and work in inclement weather.

When speculative or accepted Masonry began to take shape, the occasional Lodge such as that in which Elias Ashmole was initiated in 1646 would have been held in a suitable room at the home of one of those who took part in the ceremony.

Later, they were held in rooms at a hostelry and we know that certain furniture and effects would be used to set out the 'Lodge'. Now this is where the term Lodge varies slightly; the Lodge effects, candlesticks, hourglass, squares, compasses, etc would be loaded into a large box, known as an 'Ark' or 'Lodge' after every meeting. In Wigan there are records of this taking place in the Lodge of Sincerity during its breakaway period as an independent Lodge under the revived Antients Grand Lodge, later known as the Grand Lodge in Wigan. The 'Ark' or 'Lodge' would be moved to another hostelry when required, as was often the case.

Lodges did not begin to move into permanent buildings until the early 19th century and it is after this time that we start to see the layout change. In the Lodges which met in hostelries, members usually sat around a large table with the Master at one end and the Wardens at the other and business would be conducted with pipe smoking and beer drinking. It was the Tyler's job to supply this. Lodge accounts frequently show that money was paid out 'for liquor'.

This stopped when Lodges moved into Masonic Halls and the Lodge room started to take on the design as we know it today, symbolically oriented East to West. Why this way? Well, it was the custom to orient churches with the sepulchre in the East and as Masons were Christian men it followed that they should try, at least symbolically, to orient their Lodge rooms this way.

There is a painting in existence in the archives of the Wigan Association for Masonic Research showing the Lodge room at Leader Buildings in King Street, Wigan's first Masonic Hall, when this was occupied by the Lodge of Sincerity when it was on the roll of the Grand Lodge in Wigan. It clearly shows an intermediate layout with a central long table with candlesticks, surrounded by chairs as had been the custom; however, there are also three pedestals just as we have them now, each with a candlestick alongside it.

Finally, the term 'Lodge' has four meanings: the medieval Lodge, the Lodge or Ark box or trunk, a gathering of Masons and finally our Lodges as we know them today.

The Lodge Mentor

Mentoring is not something new; it has been used in industry and commerce for many years and there are even National Standards of Mentoring laid down in the UK. Companies run intensive induction courses for new employees and this continues with other training courses and coaching to assist the employee to achieve the standards required by the company. Incidentally, mentoring can be traced back to the ancient Greeks and the term mentor is mentioned in Homer's *Odyssey*.

As far as Freemasonry is concerned it is a fairly recent innovation and one which has now been formally recognised by the decision of the United Grand Lodge of England to make the office of Mento, a Lodge office coming immediately before the Senior Deacon. The approved badge of office is two chisels in saltire.

A Mentor according to *Chambers Dictionary* is '*a wise counsellor; a tutor; a trainer; a more senior or experienced colleague appointed to help and advise a junior colleague (business)*'.

That definition can most certainly be applied to Freemasonry when very often the mystery of our symbolism and the complexity of our ceremonies and ritual are often very confusing to the new Mason and of course it is the Lodge Mentor's duty to de-mystify much of what we do. His role is to make the new entrant feel at home, to nurture him, and guide him through the intricate paths of Freemasonry, especially during the first four or five years of his membership.

In some Lodges perhaps a very senior Mason or 'father figure' may be appointed as the Mentor. He may have special knowledge of the history of the Lodge and its traditions and, with his many years of experience in the Craft, be able to answer many of the questions that may be posed. However, whether he be old or young, one thing is certain, he must be someone who has the necessary people skills to be able to communicate with a new member.

There are those of course who say it is the responsibility of the proposer and seconder of a candidate to look after him, but that is missing the point that the mentoring scheme covers a very wide area and they may not have the expertise or knowledge to explain fully to the new member the complexities of the Masonic system.

Having said that, it does not mean to say that they have no role to play; we all have a role to play. The rest of the members of a Lodge cannot just sit back and leave it all to the Mentor. Mentoring is for everyone, regardless of age or seniority; we all need at least one person to be there for us if needed and if we have been given a job to do, a helping hand or a friendly ear can make all the difference.

Freemasonry can play a very important part in our lives and many are inspired by its high standards of integrity, honesty and the care it shows for others in the community. So when a candidate comes along we need to take care of him so that he can enjoy his Freemasonry and if he does enjoy it, that he might encourage others to join him. Think how you felt when you joined. It was all very strange at first, and we all need to be supported. The new entrant may want to know, why do we do this? or why do we that? and we need to be able answer his questions. The days are gone when the answer was 'Oh you'll find out soon enough.' That, as an answer, is no longer good enough if we wish to recruit and retain quality men in Freemasonry.

Quality matters, both quality of candidates and quality of ritual; and high standards throughout will keep good men. Mentoring is about quality and ensuring our Brethren understand why they have joined Freemasonry, what they can do for it, how it can help them, and, vitally, the reasons why they should stay as members of their Lodge.

In addition to the Lodge Mentor many Provinces have appointed Provincial Grand Mentors and when that is broken down further there may be District, Group or Divisional Mentors who look after other Mentors in a particular area.

Please give your Lodge Mentor all the support you can.

Recommended further reading: *The Lodge Mentor* by Richard Johnson, Lewis Masonic ISBN 978 085318 339 6

The Mark Degree

Some of you will have heard of the Mark Degree but may wonder what it is. Some of you will be members of it. For those who are not, let us take a look.

Under the English Constitution, the Mark degree operates under its own Grand Lodge, the Grand Lodge of Mark Master Masons of England and its Districts and Lodges Overseas; however, in Scotland, Ireland, the USA and New Zealand it is an integral part of the route from the Craft to the Royal Arch.

In England, to become a Royal Arch Mason you do not need to take the Mark Degree; however, in the Constitutions mentioned above you do. It is a step

A Mark Master Mason's apron.
Note the colours of the Craft and
the Royal Arch.

after the fellowcraft degree and has operative masonic connections. Its story is about a young fellow-craft who produces a stone for King Solomon's Temple of great skill and beauty which is much admired but rejected and thrown away. Inadvertently, he attempts to claim the wages of a more skilled workman for which he is not qualified. He is caught and punishment is demanded, but the Master of the Lodge decides that he did so without fully understanding what he was doing and allows him to go free. The moral lesson is: do not attempt to gain something to which you are not entitled.

The operative connection is clear, for there are three fellow-crafts, two of whom have produced square or oblong stones for inspection, but the third mentioned beforehand has produced a stone displaying superior skill. This stone is eventually required for a very important part of the building and would normally have been produced by a more experienced workman - as there were two kinds of masons, 'square' masons and 'round' or 'arch' masons, the latter able to demonstrate greater skill. Hence, the sign of the 'square' and the 'compasses'.

Symbolically, the connection with the Royal Arch is that the young craftsman had not yet become a Master Mason and was not qualified to preside over a Lodge of operative masons, as at one time only those who had been the Master of a Lodge were allowed to proceed to the Royal Arch. Also, the work which the craftsman had produced would eventually be recognised as one of the most important stones used in the building of the Temple, a fact which does not become apparent until you are exalted into the Royal Arch.

Various forms of the Mark Degree were worked in England from the mid-1700s, usually under a Craft Warrant, following the fellow-craft degree with a Mark Master in the Chair. The Royal Arch was given more importance by the Antients Grand Lodge and the Mark was worked regularly by their followers; however, in the Moderns not quite so much. At the time of the Union of the two

Grand Lodges in 1813 the 'Mark' became 'detached' and although occasionally still worked under a Craft Warrant, by 1818, when the Royal Arch was placed under the control of a Grand Chapter, it became even more isolated and was not seen by the new United Grand Lodge as being essential at all.

Attempts were made to make the degree an integral part of the Craft but these failed and eventually in 1861 the Grand Lodge of Mark Master Masons was formed and it is now the most successful Degree after the Craft and the Royal Arch.

In most areas of England there will be at least one Mark Lodge. The criteria for eligibility is to be a Master Mason of a regular and recognised Craft Lodge. To be Worshipful Master, a Brother should have served as the WM of a Craft Lodge - although dispensations are allowed for those who have not.

The Masonic Apron

Much has been written about the Masonic apron and several Brethren have tried to introduce some fanciful symbolism about the design of the Master Mason's in particular. Is there any symbolism in the modern apron? The answer as far as I am concerned is 'none'.

The apron is a very common piece of clothing worn by various trades and was not exclusive to the mason trade by any means. In the early days of Freemasonry all aprons were made of white leather and unadorned.

When the first Grand Lodge was formed in 1717, Grand Officers were permitted to line their aprons with blue silk and Masters and Wardens of some Lodges to line theirs with white silk. Grand Stewards of the year were allowed to line theirs with red silk.

Later, aprons began to have various designs painted on them and would often bear the symbols of a variety of degrees or orders. These were highly

A silk apron c. 1780.

decorative and incorporated many symbols such as the Square and Compasses, the All-Seeing Eye, the Sun and Moon, stars, comets, squares, levels, plumb-rule, Noah's Ark, the Anchor, the Beehive and many more.

The design with which we are familiar today did not emerge until after the Union of the two Grand Lodges in 1813. Now all aprons are standard throughout the English Constitution.

Some have tried to associate the seven tassels on an Installed Master's apron as being related to the seven liberal arts and sciences, but they are simply regalia manufacturers' representations of the fringed ends of ribbons which once secured a Brother's apron. The rosettes have also been suggested as representing the Sun, but all this is pure speculation. The so-called 'levels' of a Master's apron are described in our *Constitutions* as *'perpendicular lines upon horizontal lines, thereby forming three several sets of two right angles'* and nowhere does it refer to them as 'levels'.

Our aprons are standardised; light blue for Master Masons and Installed Masters, garter blue for Provincial and Grand Officers.

A highly decorated Craft apron of 1798. Each individual was allowed to decorate his own apron prior to 1813.

In Scotland, the colour for Grand Officers is thistle green, whilst private Lodges may wear any colour or combination of colours or tartans designed specifically for each Lodge.

In Ireland, all aprons - with the exception of an EA or FC - are light blue including Grand Officers. The point of the flap is squared off. They have different insignia for a Mason who has been installed into the Chair of a Lodge.

Whatever the constitution, we must remember that they are all white underneath all the decoration.

Many other fraternal societies wear aprons as part of their ritual, including the Oddfellows, the Buffaloes, the Free Gardeners, the Foresters and others. Many are highly decorated - much more so than those of the Freemasons from whom they took the idea.

The Office of Chaplain

The office of Chaplain in a Lodge is in some ways a strange one. The Chaplain takes precedence immediately after the Immediate Past Master who incidentally is not an officer of the Lodge - and yet the Chaplain is only an 'additional officer'.

According to the Book of Constitutions Rule 104 (a): 'The regular officers of a Lodge shall be the Master and his two Wardens, a Treasurer, Secretary, two Deacons, an Inner Guard and a Tyler. The Master shall appoint as additional officers an Almoner and a Charity Steward, and may also appoint as additional officers, a Chaplain, a Director of Ceremonies, an ADC, an Organist, an Assistant Secretary and a Steward or Stewards and no others…' That would imply that a Chaplain was not necessary; however, I have never come across a Lodge which does not have one. This is simply one of those little quirks in Freemasonry.

The Chaplain of a Lodge need not be 'a man of the cloth'; however, a Provincial Grand Chaplain and a Grand Chaplain most certainly would be.

The Chaplain's responsibility is to give prayers at the beginning and ending of the Lodge proceedings and where appropriate during the ceremonies of Initiation, Passing, Raising and Installation. He may also say grace at the Festive Board. His badge of office is a Book on a Triangle surmounting a Glory.

Considering the fact that in the early days many Lodges would meet in hostelries it is unlikely that many would have had a Chaplain who was a man of the cloth, but as they moved into dedicated Masonic Halls they were encouraged to join the Craft to serve as Lodge Chaplains. According to Bernard Jones: 'The first Grand Chaplain was not appointed until 1775 on the occasion of the laying of the foundation stone of Freemasons Hall…' The Chaplain ranks immediately after the Junior Grand Warden and Past Junior Grand Wardens.

Certainly before the Union of the two Grand Lodges, English Masonry had a strong Christian bias and Lodges were opened and closed 'in the name of God and Holy Saint John'. That is why one can still find some Lodge Installation meetings referred to as the 'Festival of St. John'. The two dates are 24 June for St. John the Baptist and 27 December for St. John the Evangelist.

Under the Grand Lodge of Scotland, a Senior Grand Chaplain ranks immediately after the GDC followed by Junior Gr. Chaplain. They also have a Grand Bible Bearer.

In Ireland, the Grand Chaplain ranks immediately after the Grand Secretary and they also have Junior Grand Chaplains.

Finally, in the USA, each Lodge has a Chaplain who is an 'additional' officer. The layout of their Lodges is different to the English Constitution, but generally the Chaplain would be seated at the eastern end of the Lodge to the left and in front of the Worshipful Master.

The Royal Arch

Many of you will be members of the Royal Arch but some of you may not - and perhaps wonder what it is. Put simply, it is not a Degree but the completion of the Third Craft Degree. The 'dDclaration' in the *Book of Constitutions* reads: '*Pure Antient Masonry consists of three Degrees and no more, viz, those of the Entered Apprentice, the Fellow Craft and the Master Mason, including the Supreme Order of the Holy Royal Arch.*'

The Order of the Royal Arch is controlled by the Supreme Grand Chapter of England with subordinate Chapters meeting under the number of a Craft Lodge. They wear separate regalia and have their own structure including Provincial and Grand Ranks.

Formerly, the Royal Arch was restricted to Masters and Past Masters, which as Bernard E. Jones says in his book '*Freemason's Guide and Compendium*', must have proved unworkable, if only because it severely restricted the number of eligible candidates. Today, a Master Mason in England of one month's standing is eligible to be 'Exalted' into the Order.

The legend of the Royal Arch in England centres around the rebuilding of the Temple, whereas in Ireland it centres around the restructuring of the Temple.

In the English ritual, we have Zerubbabel, Prince of the People; Haggai, the Prophet; and Joshua, the High Priest, whereas in the Irish version we have Josiah, the King; Hilkiah, the Priest; and Shaphan the Scribe. In America the basic legend is the same as in England, although to become a Royal Arch

A Royal Arch Companion's apron.

Mason there you must pass through four grades: Mark Mason, Past Master, Most Excellent Master and the Royal Arch. The same applies in Scotland.

The Royal Arch is said to be the completion of the Third Degree, which as most of us know refers to *'that which was lost'* and it *'repairs that loss'* through the discovery of certain secrets in a hidden vault.

Harry Carr says: *'… to all intents and purposes, the genuine secrets were lost by the death of Hiram Abiff and this resulted in the adoption of certain "substituted" secrets. This is the essence of the legend in a nutshell and the solution to the problem actually appears in the Royal Arch Ceremony where the candidate learns the precise nature of the cooperation (of the three GMs) during his entrusting. In effect our MM legend is incomplete so far as the candidate is concerned until he has taken the Royal Arch.'* Effectively, half the story is in one degree and the remainder in a later ceremony.

Harry Carr goes on to say: *'It is perfectly clear that our Third Degree legend in its present form is deliberately shaped so as to link it with an essential element in the Royal Arch, which suggests the remote possibility that originally the whole story was included in the Third Degree, so that the loss of the secrets and their subsequent recovery might have formed a single ceremony.'*

As the Grand Secretary of the Antients Grand Lodge once said, the Royal Arch is *'the root, heart and marrow of Freemasonry'* and some would say that no Mason has completed his Third Degree until he is Exalted into the Royal Arch.

Please contact your Royal Arch representative if you wish to know more.

The Seven Liberal Arts and Sciences

We hear these mentioned in the Second Degree and although they are briefly outlined, what are they? A few hundred years ago they formed the curriculum of all the major universities.

The first is Grammar, followed by Rhetoric, then Logic, Arithmetic, Geometry, Music and finally Astronomy.

Let us take a look at them individually. They are described in the fourth section of the Second Emulation Lecture, somewhat abbreviated for this paper:

Grammar teaches the proper arrangement of work...and that of excellence of punctuation which enable us to speak and write language with accuracy and precision, agreeable to reason, authority and strict rules of literature.

Rhetoric teaches us to speak copiously and fluently on any subject...with all the advantages of force and elegance...

Logic teaches us to guide our reason...and to direct our enquiries after truth...it consists of regular trains of argument whence we infer, deduce and conclude...in it are employed the faculties of conceiving, reasoning, judging and disposing...

Arithmetic teaches the powers and properties of numbers...by this art, reasons and demonstrations are given for finding any certain number whose relation...to another number is already discovered.

Geometry treats of the powers and properties of magnitude in general, where length and breadth, or length, breadth and thickness are considered.

Music teaches us the art of forming concords, so as to produce a delightful harmony...it enquires into the nature of concords and discords and enables us to find out a true proportion between them...

Astronomy is that divine art by which we are taught to read the wisdom, strength and beauty of the Almighty Creator in the sacred pages of the celestial hemisphere...by it also we learn the ...primary laws of nature; and while we are employed in the study of this science, we may perceive unparalleled instances of wisdom and goodness.

They can be found in full in *The Little Green Book* better known as the *Lectures of the Three Degrees in Craft Masonry*. I would recommend that you buy this little book for there is much within which will help you with your Freemasonry. Copies can be obtained from any Masonic regalia supplier.

The Sign of Fidelity and Sign of Reverence

During the Second Degree, we are shown the Sign of Fidelity as part of the signs of that Degree and the Sign of Fidelity is explained thus: *'p.t.r.h.on.t.l b.w.t.t.e.i.t.f.o.a.s. emblematically to shield the repository of your secrets from the attacks of the insidious'.*

This is a sign with which many of us all familiar, but what about the Sign of Reverence or Prayer? It mentions it at the point of prayer as the candidate enters in the First Degree and also on entry in the Second and Third, but - what is it? It can often be seen when the Chaplain gives the prayer at the opening and closing of the Lodge and sometimes during that part of a ceremony when a candidate is giving his obligation. The difference between the S of Fidelity and the S of Prayer is the position of the thumb.

In the former it is erect and in the latter alongside the fingers. So if the latter is not described in any ritual where did it come from? That is a very good question and one to which I don't have a full answer, but it was certainly the subject of some debate during the mid-20th century.

The late Dr. E. H. Cartwright, a very knowledgeable Mason and expert ritualist, was scathing of the practice of using the so-called 'Sign of Prayer' in his book *Masonic Ritual* published in 1947. He claimed: '*In a discussion on the subject some years ago in "Miscellanea Latomorum", a brother actually admitted that the 'sign of prayer is not taught in any Lodge but in Lodges of Instruction'. That stultifies his support of its use, for no Lodge of Instruction has the right to invent and to teach any sign that is not taught in the course of recognised ceremonies. The attitude of this so-called Sign of Reverence or Prayer is not even suggestive of either the quality or the act. It is suggestive of fidelity and secrecy and is, indeed, used in that sense as part of a sign used in the Royal Arch.*'

He went on to say: '*Present-day practice varies so much that one must be content to copy the actions of the members of the Lodge in which one finds oneself; however, undoubtedly the correct (as being rational and certainly older) method is to use the sign of the Degree during prayers and that of Fidelity during obligations, the latter of course being retained until after the formal sealing.*'

So where did it come from? I don't suppose we will ever know; it is like a lot of other things in Freemasonry which have become 'custom and practice' over time.

So should we use it? If your Lodge uses it regularly and it has become the custom in your Lodge to do so, then you are likely to follow suit.

It is one of the little quirks of Freemasonry which make it so interesting. Wouldn't it be boring if everything was the same wherever we went?

The Symbolism of the Key

Harry Carr in *The Freemason at Work* says: '*Apart from the three virtues, there is one more symbol which appears regularly on or near the Ladder, on the First Degree Tracing Board and that is the "Key".*' Josiah Bowring, for a very good reason, showed it hanging from one of the rungs on his First Degree Tracing Board. It is one of the oldest symbols of Masonry, and is mentioned in one of our earliest ritual documents, the *Edinburgh Register House MS*, of around 1696. The manuscript contains the following catechism:

'*Q. Which is the key of your Lodge?*
A. A weel hung tongue.'

Many of the early texts expanded the 'Key-Tongue' symbolism, stating that it was lodged in 'the bone box' (i.e., the mouth), and that it is the key to the Mason's secrets. But one of the best answers on this point is in the *Sloane MS* dating from around 1700, which is the earliest ritual document to contain the words '*the tongue of good report*', words which have survived in our ritual today. This particular manuscript includes the catechism:

'*Q. What is the Keys of your Lodge Doore made of?*
A. It is not made of Wood, Stone, Iron or Steel or any sort of mettle but the Tongue
    of a good report behind a brother's back as well as before his face.'

It is said that in Scotland in the 1600s, no Lodge could meet in an inhabited dwelling-house, save in ill-weather and then only in a building 'where no person shall hear or see us'. Otherwise, meetings were to be held 'in the open fields'. Aberdeen masons were said to erect a tent for the candidate's Initiation and special mention was made of 'the ancient outfield Lodge in the Parish of Negg near Loch Ness when the book of laws was securely locked in a box and carried to any place where an apprentice was to be received with "three masters of the keys" bearing three the box keys'.

The first section of the First Emulation Lecture, speaks of secrets:

'*Q. As Masons, how do we hope to get at them?*
A. By the help of a key.
Q. Does that key hang or lie?
A. It hangs.
Q. Why is the preference given to hanging?
A. It should always hang in a Brother's defence, and never lie to his prejudice.
Q. What does it hang by?
A. The thread of life, in the passage of utterance, between guttural and pectoral.
Q. Why so nearly connected to the heart?
A. Being an index of the mind, it should utter nothing but what the heart dictates.
Q. It is a curious key: of what metal is it composed?
A. No metal; it is the tongue of good report.'

Today, in English Lodges the key is the symbol of the office of Treasurer, one of the most important offices in a Lodge.

The Symbolism of the Sword

The Tyler is the outer guard of the Lodge room. The position is first referred to in Anderson's *New Book of Constitutions* in 1738. Its origin is unknown but it may have originated from protecting the roof of a building by tiling its roof. The jewel of the Tyler is the sword and his situation is outside the door of the Lodge. His duty is to be armed with a drawn sword to keep off all intruders and Cowans to Masonry.

Swords appeared on aprons in the mid-18th century, on the continent and particularly in France. The sword is usually depicted on hand-made aprons or on illustrations from the period.

One which includes swords is seen in a continental illustration probably from France, in which the candidate is lying on the floor of the Lodge room surrounded by Brethren with drawn swords pointed at him. This stems from the time when it was common for gentlemen to carry a sword. In English Masonic illustrations of the time, the sword is not generally seen.

Also in the Antients Grand Lodge, 'sentinels' with swords were used to guard the veils during the early versions of the Royal Arch ceremony.

In Irish Masonry, in the First Degree after the candidate is restored to light, his attention is directed to Brethren around the Altar. On the one hand he sees hands outstretched in welcome and fellowship; on the other, backs turned in indifference, working tools snatched up as weapons and drawn swords - warning of what he might (symbolically) expect if he were to fail to keep his undertaking. There may be a connection with the example from France quoted above.

There is a famous watercolour which depicts a lady being accepted into a Lodge of Adoption in France in the 19th century. These Lodges operated under a regular Lodge but admitted women into their ranks; however, they did not use the Masonic degrees but some others with a distinct Masonic flavour. There are ladies and gentlemen depicted in the illustration and all the men are pointing swords at the lady candidate as a blindfold is removed.

There is a further illustration from c. 1740, depicting King Frederick II of Prussia adopting Friedrich Margrave of Brandenburg-Bayreuth into Freemasonry, in which it appears that a sword is being handed to him. Others present are also carrying swords.

The sword is not used in English Masonic practice with the exception of the appointment of the Tyler and occasionally the Inner Guard at the Installation of a new Master.

In some old Lodges, the Tyler and Inner Guard may parade in front of the Master with sword and poignard or a sword each and describe their duties before the Lodge is opened.

Crossed swords are shown on aprons as the emblem of a Provincial Grand Sword Bearer and Grand Sword Bearer. Invariably a Deputy Provincial Grand Master will hold the rank of Past Grand Sword Bearer.

The Toast – The Duke of Lancaster

In most of the English Craft, the first toast at a festive board is to The Queen or to The Queen and the Craft. However, in the Provinces of West and East Lancashire another toast is given to that of The Queen – The Duke of Lancaster. Why?

There were three creations of the Duke of Lancaster. The first was on 6 March 1351, Henry of Grosmont, 4th Earl of Lancaster, a great-grandson of Henry III; he was also 4th Earl of Leicester, 1st Earl of Derby, 1st Earl of Lincoln and Lord of Bowland. This creation became extinct on the 1st Duke's death in 1361.

The second creation was on 13 November 1362, for John of Gaunt, 1st Earl of Richmond, who was both the 1st Duke's son-in-law and also fourth son of King Edward III. John had married Blanche of Lancaster, 6th Countess of Lancaster, daughter of the 1st Duke of the first creation. When John of Gaunt, the 1st Duke of this creation, died on 4 February 1399, the Dukedom passed to his son, Henry of Bolingbroke, 1st Duke of Hereford. Later that same year, the new 2nd Duke usurped the throne of England from Richard II, ascending the throne as Henry IV, at which point the Dukedom merged in the Crown.

The third creation was on 10 November 1399, for Henry of Monmouth, Prince of Wales, eldest son of the new king. In 1413, the 1st Duke ascended the throne as King Henry V, and the Dukedom merged in the Crown again.

The Duchy of Lancaster continues to exist as a separate entity from the Crown Estate and currently provides income for the monarch, Elizabeth II. The Sovereign is styled as Duke of Lancaster, regardless of gender, although it is an honorary title and a royal style. The Dukedom became extinct after Henry VI, as the original charter restricted it to 'heirs male'. Despite this, George V approved the ongoing use of the title.

It is customary at formal dinners in Lancashire and in Lancastrian regiments of the armed forces for the Loyal Toast to the Crown to be announced as 'The

Queen, Duke of Lancaster' and this is probably from where the Craft in the two Provinces adopted it.

In Lancaster it was quite common as late as the second half of the twentieth century to hear the national anthem sung as 'God save our gracious Queen, Long live our noble Duke ...'

There is another suggestion that the toast was approved by George V after a very pleasant visit to the city of Manchester, when at dinner the toast was given unofficially and which pleased the King. I have no proof of the latter statement, but the toast persists in both Masonic Provinces.

The Trouser Leg and the Breast

Why do we roll up our trouser leg? You sometimes hear people poking fun at the antics of Freemasons and this I will guarantee is the most common. Why then do we do it, you may ask. Well, there is quite a simple explanation.

Our predecessors the stonemasons did not wear long trousers like we do today; they wore knee breeches and they also wore long leather aprons to protect themselves. If a young man wanted to become an entered apprentice he first had to prove himself to his potential Master as a fit and proper person for the arduous job of being a stonemason.

Physically, he needed to show that he was male, (the breast) and that he had good arms, (the sleeve rolled up) and that his legs were sound, (the modern-day trouser leg rolled up). But in medieval times he would not need to do so as he would be wearing knee breeches.

For instance, the Cutlers Guild in 1420 insisted on the apprentice being 'of free birth and condition, handsome in stature, having straight and proper limbs'. A young man born out of wedlock would not be regarded as a fit and proper person.

So why then do we need to do it today? Well, it is a long-held tradition probably of Jewish origin that if you were making a promise on the Bible, you would take it 'on bare and bended knee' and that is the simple explanation. Just as people take their shoes off when walking into a holy place; it is a sign of respect and sincerity.

It is an ancient tradition which has been carried on for centuries, but even today in some Lodges in this country and more commonly on the continent, a candidate for Initiation was 'neither naked or clad' and was required to change into a special white suit, which has the knees exposed, the breast laid open with short sleeve so that the arms are visible. It also indicates that he is 'poor and penniless'. Not only is he required to wear a special suit but must also sit alone in a room for up to an hour before the ceremony and is required to write down on a sheet of paper his reason for wishing to become a Mason. This is sometimes known as the Chamber of Reflection.

So next time you are asked by someone: 'Why do you roll up your trouser leg?' just tell them you are following the traditions of the ancient stonemasons who when they went into church probably wore knee breeches and so knelt on a bare knee as a sign of respect.

We are simply following tradition.

The Tyler or Outer Guard

The first person most of us have any contact with at our Initiation ceremony is the Tyler of the Lodge as he prepares us for the ceremony to follow and I think you will all agree it is a strange name for an officer of the Lodge. So where does the name Tyler come from?

The name Tyler appears to have particular Masonic usage, but Tiler comes from the craft of making tiles, or from covering a roof or building with tiles. The earliest mention I can find is in Hone's *Every-Day Book* (1827): *'Two Tylers or Guarders are to guard the Lodge with a drawn sword, from all Cowans and Eves-droppers.'*

According to the late Harry Carr, Anderson, in his first *Book of Constitutions* in 1723 referred not to a Tyler but: *'Another Brother (who must be a Fellow-Craft) should be appointed to look after the door of the Grand Lodge, but shall not be a member of it.'*

In the second edition in 1738, he did use the title 'Tyler'. Eventually the term 'Tyler' came into general use; however, his duties were not just to guard the door. He had to draw the designs on the floor of the Lodge, ensure that the summons for the meeting was delivered to members and prepare the candidates.

Often a Tyler would be paid for his duties and even today in some Masonic Halls there is a permanent Tyler who will act for several Lodges.

It has been suggested that the craft of Tiler was always the last to be required at a building to cover the roof to protect it, and in a sense that is what the Masonic Tyler is doing; he is protecting the secrets of the Lodge. In a practical sense, when Lodges used to meet in rooms in hostelries, there would always be the danger of eavesdroppers and those who had perhaps taken too much drink wanting to know what the Masons were doing - and of course in those times it was common for people to carry swords.

Of the Tylers duties we hear the JW say: *'To keep off all intruders and Cowans to Masonry.'* What is a Cowan? Well the term would appear to be Scottish and

The Tyler of Royal Forest Lodge No. 401. He is formally invested with his sword and the coat at the annual Installation of the Lodge. The coat dates back to 1829.

refer to a dry stone waller, one who was less skilled than a stonemason and not allowed to use lime mortar. He was not in receipt of the 'Mason's Word'. In other words he had not served an apprenticeship and received the secret words of the skilled man. We will learn more about Cowans in another paper.

It is not uncommon in English Masonry for the Tyler to enter with the procession, carrying his sword, at the start of proceedings and recite his duties to the Master before the Lodge is formally opened. At the end he is called in before the closing and exits with the procession.

In English Lodges, the Tyler must be at least a Master Mason.

Finally, Albert G. Mackey claims that: '*As in operative masonry, the Tyler, when the edifice is erected, finishes and covers the roof, so, in speculative Masonry when the Lodge is duly organised, the Tyler closes the door, and covers the sacred precincts from all intrusion.*'

The Volume of the Sacred Law in the Lodge-Room

In Emulation practice it is common for the VSL to be facing the Master. That is, with the wording facing towards him and the Sq & C with the points towards the bottom of the page. But should it be left facing that way when a candidate is taking his obligation? How many Lodges bother to turn it round to face the candidate? Or do we even think about it? Very few do, I suspect.

Let us take a look at what the Basic Principles for Grand Lodge Recognition approved in 1929 - and still in force - say on the subject:

> '3. That all Initiates shall take their Obligation on or in full view of the open Volume of the Sacred Law, by which is meant the revelation from above which is binding on the conscience of the particular individual who is being initiated.'

That would imply, to my thinking, that the candidate should be able to recognise it and read it. This problem would not occur in Scotland, Ireland or the USA, for in their Constitutions the pedestal or altar is in the centre of the room at which the candidate kneels and as such the VSL is always arranged to face the candidate.

Harry Carr mentions in *Freemason at Work* that in the Grand Lodge of New Zealand it is the practice of the Lodge to have one volume facing the Master and another smaller volume presented to the Initiate, which is placed in front of him on the pedestal between him and the larger VSL, facing him whenever he takes an obligation in any of the three degrees.

Peter Hamilton Currie, a PM of Quatuor Coronati Lodge of Masonic Research, wrote to the author of this paper in answer to a query on this subject, advising that under 'Stability' working in England the current ritual book reads as follows: *'No object should ever be placed on the V of SL except the S & C's. The V of the SL should be placed facing the candidate, and the Ps of C's should point towards the bottom of the page.'* He also brought my attention to regulation 155 of the *B of C* which states: *'The members present at any Lodge duly summoned have an undoubted right to regulate their own proceedings, provided that they are consistent with the general laws and regulations of the Craft etc etc...'*

So it is actually up to each Lodge to decide. Some will leave it as it is and others may decide to turn round the VSL every time an obligation is being taken, or as Peter Hamilton Currie's Lodge does for each candidate when a small VSL is placed near the large Volume - both facing the candidate.

Exposures of old Masonic ritual do reveal the manner in which Obligations were taken, with the candidate placing his right hand on the VSL, while supporting it with his left, a position in which one would assume that he himself ought to be able to read it. This is reflected in the Scottish Due Guard.

Perhaps this is something Lodges ought to address?

The Wardens

Along with the Master of a Lodge, the Wardens derive from the old guild system and are appointed to assist the Master in the ruling and governing of the Lodge. In the English guilds, it was not uncommon for there to be Senior and Junior Wardens or Upper and Lower Wardens.

Today a Brother must have served as a Warden for a full year to be eligible to become the Master of a Lodge. The Junior Warden is responsible for ensuring that visitors are regularly made Masons.

In the English Constitution there is a stipulation that a Brother who is invested as a Warden at the regular Installation meeting, but who does not attend any subsequent meetings, is qualified to be elected Master, whereas a Brother who was absent at the Installation, but has attended and carried out his duties at every meeting since, is not qualified.

However, if a Brother has only served part of a year as Warden, he may be rendered eligible to be elected as Master by a Dispensation of the Provincial Grand Master under Rule 109, but only on a petition giving the reason for the delay in his investiture, his actual service as a Warden and the special reason why a dispensation is sought. This rule only applies to a Brother who has short service as a Warden.

Unlike today where the Wardens sit at pedestal in the West and South, the Wardens in the very old Lodges would be seated at a table in the triangular form with the Master at one end and the Wardens at the other and Brethren seated in order of seniority to the sides. Alternatively, when the table had been dispensed with, both Wardens could be found sitting in the West, Junior on the left and Senior on the right.

In the speculative Lodges of the eighteenth century the Wardens did not always have pedestals; there would probably have been two tall pillars on the floor of the Lodge. These have now been replaced by the two columns on their pedestal in front of them.

In the Lodge of Sincerity, when it was No.1 on the roll of the Grand Lodge in Wigan, now No. 3677, the layout was a combination of a long central table with chairs around it, but with three pedestals as they are now situated. This would appear to signify a transitional period for the layout of a Lodge.

Today, when the Lodge is opened and the IPM has opened the VSL, the Junior Warden lowers the column on his pedestal and Senior Warden raises his. The reverse takes place when the Lodge is being closed.

The Worshipful Master

Some of our detractors have picked up on the word 'Worshipful' as being unreligious or somehow wrong. The dictionary definition of the word 'worshipful' is given as: *'Worthy of worship or honour; Used as a term of respect in addressing certain dignitaries'*. The sense in which we use it is as a term of respect for the honour the Brother has had bestowed on him as Master of his Lodge and not to 'worship' him any way.

When speculative Masonry began there were only two degrees, that of Entered Apprentice and that of Fellow of the Craft. It was not until around 1732 that we first hear of a third degree and the term Master Mason. This is not to say that a Master Mason was the same thing as the Master of a Lodge - in fact for some time the Worshipful Master of a Lodge would be selected from the 'Fellows'.

There was not an Installation ceremony as we now know it; a Master was elected and simply placed in the Chair of the Lodge without any esoteric ceremony being involved or any additional secrets being conferred. When the Antients Grand Lodge came along in 1751, initially there was no 'Installation' ceremony as such, and certainly the rival Moderns Grand Lodge didn't have one either - at least not until around 1770 and then not of all their Lodges held an esoteric ceremony. On the other hand, we know from a Masonic exposé that the Antients did have one from about 1760 onwards.

In those early days it was not uncommon for a Master to serve for only six months and often they would be re-elected and served for long periods. Nowadays, it is customary for there to be an Installation every year. This was only formalised in 1827, several years after the Union of the two Grand Lodges.

There are still some Lodges which work an extended form of the Installation ceremony which has additional signs and passwords, but it is not necessary for an Installed Master under the English Craft to receive them or to partake in the additional ceremonial.

To be the Master of a Lodge a Brother must have served as a Warden for at least a year (explained in my paper about the Wardens) and he must have been proposed and so elected by the members of his Lodge present at the meeting generally held the month before the Installation ceremony.

A Master may not serve more than two years consecutively except by special dispensation, which is only given if there are special circumstances to warrant it. One Brother from Wigan, Henry Miller, from the Lodge of Antiquity, had the distinction of serving as Master of his Lodge no fewer than twelve times during the 1800s and this is not far from being a record - only beaten by two others who served once and twice more. When a Master has served his year he becomes a Past Master with the title Worshipful Brother.

Dr. Oliver once said: *'The WM should always bear in his memory that to him the Brethren look for instruction – on him depends the welfare and success, the credit and popularity of the community. His situation as the chief pillar of the Lodge is most important; and if he fail in the satisfactory discharge of its duties, he inflicts a fatal blow, not only on the Lodge, which will be the first victim of an ill-placed confidence, but on the order of Freemasonry itself...'*

To Keep Off All Intruders and Cowans to Masonry

How many times have we heard those words uttered by the Junior Warden in answer to the Worshipful Master's question. Some of us will have heard them hundreds of times but there are undoubtedly some who may wonder what they mean.

Chambers Dictionary gives us one of several definitions of the word 'intruder' but the one most appropriate is: *'A person who enters premises secretly or by force.'* I think that needs no further explanation, but what about the other word: 'Cowan', now that's a little different.

Chambers again: *'A dry-stone diker, a mason* [with a small 'm'] *who has never served an apprenticeship; someone who tries to enter a Freemasons' Lodge surreptitiously.'*

However, some Lodges use the words *'Cowans and Evesdroppers to Masonry'*, particularly those which use the Stability, Logic, Universal or West End workings.

The word 'cowan' is a Scottish trade term, a dry stone waller, one who was not allowed to use lime mortar - and here is a connection with our operative past. A cowan was not as skilled as other masons and in Scotland in the strictly controlled trade bodies, as he had not served an apprenticeship, he was not allowed to know the secrets of the Lodge or receive the 'Mason's Word.'

According to the late Harry Carr in his book *The Freemason at Work*, a Cowan in operative times was certainly an intruder, from the trade point of view: he could not have learned very much of the trade if he merely listened under the eaves. In speculative Masonry it is likely the eavesdropper, the secret listener, would be a great source of danger.

The evesdropper form of ritual came first and the earliest appearance of 'cowans or evesdroppers' is in Prichard's *Masonry Dissected*, a published exposure of Masonic ritual in 1730:

'Q. Where stands the Junior Entered Apprentice?
A. In the north.
Q. And what is his business?
A. To keep off all Cowans and Evesdroppers.'

Carr continues by saying: '*Another question followed, implying that our Brethren in those days were very willing to let the punishment fit the crime:*

Q. If a Cowan (or listener) is catched, how is he to be punished?
A. To be placed under the eaves of the house, (in rainy weather) till the water runs in at his shoulders and out of his shoes.'

In Emulation working it is always '*Cowans and Intruders*'.

Thus, this is where the term 'Cowan' comes from. I suppose the modern parallel in the building trade today is somebody who could be regarded as a 'Cowboy'!

Tracing Boards

Why do we have Tracing Boards in the Lodge and what are they for?

Our modern-day Tracing Boards are descendants of old practices carried out in our early Lodges, that of drawing on the floor of the Lodge symbols used in the ceremonies. However, there was an earlier use of Tracing Boards, that of the Master Mason or Architect who set out his plans for the building, examples of which can still be found in York Minster.

In the early speculative Lodges, it was usually the Tyler's duty to draw a design on the floor with chalk and the latest apprentice's task to erase with mop and pail after the meeting finished.

Later, along came floor-cloths with elaborate designs and symbols usually representative of all three degrees. Many still exist and locally they can be found in Macclesfield, Congleton, Kendal and Swinton, Manchester. These are now highly prized items among a Lodge's artefacts and are carefully preserved for the future.

Our modern-day Tracing Boards came along in the early 1800s and the designs vary from one artist to another but probably one of the first was Josiah

Forerunner to Tracing Board: a Floorcloth
Second Degree from Swinton, Manchester,
measures 89¾in x 44in or 2280mm x
1120mm.

Bowring who introduced three female figures into the First Degree TB, those of Faith, Hope and Charity, standing on a ladder leading to the Heavens. Some later boards had these omitted, but the current First Degree TB, which most Lodges use, has the three female figures depicted standing on what appears to be a staircase. Also, we have the three great pillars of Wisdom, Strength and Beauty.

Over the years there have been many different designs with varying symbols and it is interesting to see those variations when visiting different Lodges and also their location in the in the Lodge-room.

In my Lodge we have ours located in front of the three pedestals; some Lodges have them on the chequered carpet, one on top of the other, and some have them on the wall of the Lodge-room covered by curtains or doors which are opened and closed at the appropriate point during the work of the Lodge.

You will have noticed that it is the Deacon's responsibility to attend to the Tracing Boards. In my own Lodge, the Junior Deacon does the First and Second degrees, and the Senior Deacon the Third degree.

Their use today is purely symbolic and from time to time you will hear the lectures given in open Lodge on all three boards.

Overseas, their use varies; some constitutions have them whilst others do not. For instance they are invariably not used in the USA, neither are they used in Ireland. Some Scottish Lodges use them in a similar way to England but this is by no means universal. Copies of all three Tracing Boards are reproduced in the Emulation Ritual book.

Julian Rees, in his book *Tracing Boards of the Three Degrees in Craft Freemasonry Explained* states: '*Why tracing boards? Well we can find rich justification for them from within the Masonic ritual itself. Historically, too, we find accounts of our forebears tracing symbols on the floor of the Lodge room, a practice that became codified and then embellished later to produce some examples of truly outstanding artistic achievement…*'

What Happened to the Trowel?

The trowel featured prominently in Freemasonry prior to the union of the two Grand Lodges in 1813, but then it seemed to disappear. What happened to it?

The trowel is a working tool used to bind brickwork or stonework with cement when a building is being erected, so in masonic terms it is a tool used *after* the mason had cut the stone and perhaps one which a stonemason would not use. Is this the reason for its relative disappearance from speculative Freemasonry?

In the early 18th century, the trowel may have played more of a part in our ceremonies - at one time the Inner Guard's instrument was a trowel. In Frederick Smyth's *A Reference Book for Freemasons* he claims that it was a tool of great importance to the operative mason and then goes on to say: '*In The Grand Mystery Laid Open, an exposure of 1726, the candidate holds a hammer and trowel.*' He also says that it was the badge of an Entered Apprentice and still is in some places.

In Bernard Jones' book *Freemasons Guide and Compendium,* he points out that '*in Carmarthen in Wales there is a record of a Lodge which paid for "5 Trowells and mending 12 others"*'. This seems to suggest that in that old Lodge the trowel had a considerable part to play.

The trowel also features on the Banner of the Royal Order of Scotland, where it is shown on the right side being held upright by a hand. On the opposite side is the sword in a hand. It is also depicted in the jewel of the Deputy Grand Master, Governor and Provincial Grand Masters of the Order.

In Bristol it still features in their ceremonies, where I understand it plays a part in the First and Third Degrees. We must not forget that Freemasons in that city retained many of the old features lost to most at the time of the Union.

In Scotland, the trowel is the badge of the Grand Junior Deacon and of course under the English Constitution it is the badge of the Charity Steward.

In the Ancient Charge delivered to the candidate after Initiation we say those famous words: '*Monarchs themselves have not found it derogatory to exchange the Sceptre for the trowel.*'

I suggest it means little to many Brethren because of the lack of references to the trowel elsewhere in our ritual. However, the trowel does reappear briefly in Emulation working as one of the working tools of an Installed Master.

Bernard Jones again mentions Social Lodge of Norwich who still invest their Initiates with a silver trowel, with which they are exhorted: '*emblematically to stop up all interstices in the Lodge so that not a sound shall escape from within, nor an eye pry without.*'

Here is an old piece of ritual regarding the trowel:

> '*The working tools of a Freemason are all the implements of Masonry indiscriminately; but more especially the trowel. The trowel is an instrument made use of by operative masons, to spread the cement which unites a building into one common mass; but we, as free and accepted and speculative Masons, are taught to make use of it for the more noble and glorious purpose of spreading brotherly love and affection, that cement which unites us into one sacred band, or society of friends and brothers, among whom no contention should ever exist, but that noble contention, or rather emulation, of who can best work and best agree.*'

What is a Lewis?

In Freemasonry, the term 'Lewis' has a double symbolic meaning: firstly as the son of a Mason and secondly as a device by which stone may be lifted during the erection of a building.

According to Bernard E. Jones in his *Freemasons' Guide and Compendium* a Lewis in the building sense: '*...is a grapnel, for which a specially shaped socket needs to be cut in the top face of the block of hard, strong stone that is to be lifted... Two opposite sides or ends of the socket are undercut ..two projecting wedge shaped, tapered steel keys are introduced into the socket, and between them is inserted a parallel steel spacer which spreads the wedges into the undercut parts; then a shackle pin, or bolt, is passed through the upper extensions of all three, and provides a hold for the lifting chain.*'

These can often be seen on the floor of Lodges fixed in the Perfect Ashlar hanging from a derrick.

In the Masonic sense, a Lewis is the uninitiated son of a Mason and it matters not whether the son was born before or after his father became a Mason. In English Masonry a Lewis's sole privilege is that of being entitled by custom when there is more than one candidate on the same day to be initiated first. He cannot claim precedence over candidates proposed or elected previously to him, and he must take his place in the usual rotation of any waiting list. Being a Lewis is not grounds for dispensation to enable him to be initiated under the age of 21. (Rule 157, *B of C*)

See *Information for the Guidance of Members of the Craft.*

Bernard Jones again: '*There is a late 18th century poem which goes as follows:*

Q. What do we call the son of a Freemason?

A. A Lewis.

Q. What does that denote?

A. Strength.

Q. How is a lewis depicted in a Mason's Lodge?

A. As a cramp of metal (etc).

Q. What is duty of a Lewis…to his aged parent?

A. To bear the heavy burden … so as to render the close of their days happy and comfortable.

Q. His privilege for doing so?

A. To be made a Mason before any other person, however dignified by birth, rank or riches, unless he, through complaisance, waives his privilege.

Under the Scottish Constitution, the son of a Master Mason owing allegiance to the Grand Lodge of Scotland may seek Initiation at any time after he has reached the age of 18. Also in Australia a similar rule applies.

In American Lodges, a Lewis is generally not known, although Harry Carr in *Freemason at Work* mentions a Lodge of French origin in New York having a non-Masonic ceremony during which the son of a Brother is recognised; this is termed a Baptism. Often they are introduced at a very young age and a savings account may be opened for him to be paid out at 21.

What Is The Usual Manner Observed Amongst Masons?

We often hear the WM say: '*Brethren, 'You have all heard the proposition, I will now ask you to vote in the usual manner observed amongst Masons.'*

But for the less experienced Brethren, let me explain. There are two methods of voting in a Lodge. The first is by ballot, using white and black balls. White for and black against. These are usually taken round by the Deacons and given to each member and collected afterwards after the Master has announced the result.

Another method certainly employed in Middlesex is to use a voting box with two drawers, the Yes drawer and the Nay drawer. The Deacons give each member a ball (the colour does not matter) and they put the ball in either drawer, Yes for in favour of the vote and Nay against. Before and after the vote the WM displays the Nay drawer to show that it is empty. If, after the vote, it contains more than two balls, the vote is against.

The second method is by a show of hands and it is that which I will discuss in greater detail below.

What is the method of voting prescribed by Grand Lodge? By a resolution of the Premier Grand Lodge in 1736 it was agreed that *'The concurrence or dissent of the members is always to be signified by holding up one of their hands.'* It did not, however, define the word 'up'.

The Antients Grand Lodge in its Constitutions in 1756 used the words: *'The opinions, or votes of the members, are to be signified by the holding up of hands; that is one hand of each member…'*

The first *Book of Constitutions of United Grand Lodge* had the words *'The votes of members are always to be signified by each holding up one of his hands.'*

So the current *Book of Constitutions* Rule 59 *says 'that the votes are to be signified by each member holding up one hand.'*

All of these examples are referring to votes in Grand Lodge. Nothing is said about votes in private Lodges, so the answer is probably in the Rule 59 of the *Book of Constitutions.*

However, I was asked this question some time ago and one Brother suggested to me that the reason we hold out our hand in a horizontal manner is meant to represent the right hand on the VSL, but I am not convinced that that explanation has any credence.

My honest opinion is that the reason we do what we do is lost in the mists of time and that it has become custom and practice in the Province of West Lancashire to hold the hand in the horizontal manner but I have been elsewhere when the sign is given in the manner of the right hand held in up in the form of a square. In the North-East this is often accompanied by the words *'Whi aye Man'.*

I think the jury is still out on this one, unless someone can offer another explanation.

When and Where Did Freemasonry Start? – Part 1

If I could give a definitive answer to that question in a five-minute paper I think I would become famous, but I shall do my best to give you more food for thought!

There have been thousands of words written about the supposed beginnings of Freemasonry in England. Even today we do not really know how, when or where it started; however, I will put forward some suggestions.

The first history of the Craft was written by the Rev. Dr. James Anderson for the first Grand Lodge in 1723. Much of what Anderson wrote was an attempt to create a history for his newly formed Grand Lodge and has since been criticised by various scholars, but as John Hamill has stated in his book *The Craft* he was not trying to write an authentic history but rather an honourable history for a new institution.

He claimed that Freemasons' Lodges had existed from ancient times and also stated that Prince Edwin, having called a great assembly of masons at York in AD 926, had granted them a Constitution and ordered them to meet quarterly to regulate their Lodges.

Anderson wrote an even more elaborate story from the time of Edwin to the date of the formation of the new Grand Lodge in 1717, and included numerous personalities as masons for which no evidence exists. Since then Masonic historians have tended to disregard his writings as figments of an overactive mind.

So what of the other theories? One which has gained increasing favour over the past few years is the transition from the operative (working) masons to speculative or accepted masons as having evolved from the guild system. Direct evidence is, however, hard to come by and historians have been searching for this for many years.

Working masons were involved in the building of the many great cathedrals and abbeys and would occupy a 'lodge' which was erected at the side of the building. This is where they would work, eat and sleep throughout the many years it would take to complete the building. However, these masons, although religious men, did not have a speculative side to their organisation. They were employed by the clergy or even the monarch and were paid wages fixed by their masters.

It is not until we get to the 1500s and 1600s that we see something akin to a speculative element emerging, but that does not mean there was a direct transition from operative to speculative Masonry.

A theory put forward is that in this period, a time of unrest in the country which would eventually lead to a civil war, men of like mind who were fed up with the intolerance shown by the state and religious bodies wanted to be able to improve society in a time when any gathering of men would be considered subversive. They wanted to be able to meet together to promote tolerance to achieve a better society and to be able to follow their conscience in matters of religion and politics, and it is from this that speculative Freemasonry emerged.

This is just one theory and in the next part we will look at how a change from operative to speculative may have taken place.

When and Where Did Freemasonry Start? – Part 2

We left off in Part 1 in the 1500-1600s and the theory that some men who were disillusioned with the political and religious intolerance of the times began to come together with the common aim of social improvement. Such views, though, would at the time have been considered subversive. One method of avoiding this charge would have been to adopt the guise of a builder's organisation or a guild in which they could meet to discuss their ideas.

Another theory is that of a self-help group meeting at a suitable tavern where members of various trades would pay a fee at every meeting, which would go into a common pot for distribution to those in need. We must remember that there was no state welfare or National Health Service in those days, and those who became sick or fell on hard times had to rely on local charity.

These became known as the Box Clubs. Each trade had its own club, but eventually they began to accept members who were not tradesmen and it is known that in Scotland the operative Lodges admitted non-craftsmen into their ranks as early as 1600. There is ample evidence to show this.

The Rev V. W. Bro. Neville Barker Cryer in his book *York Mysteries Revealed* has pointed out that trade guilds, including the masons, were sponsoring and performing mystery plays in York by 1378. However, by 1540, several guilds had disappeared - but the trade guilds had survived. He also pointed out that when the destruction of the monasteries took place during the mid-sixteenth century, much of the work which stonemasons would have carried out had gone and by then non-operatives were being admitted into their Lodges.

He has found evidence that non-masons were admitted into masons' guilds from at least 1569. The operative stonemasons gradually grew into chartered companies, leaving the old guild Lodges as 'private' Lodges. His conclusion was that a form of non-operative Masonry was in existence in York by about 1600, employing a set of old charges used by operative masons, which were now involving non-operative members, well before Ashmole's Initiation at Warrington in 1646.

For Ashmole to have been initiated into a Lodge in Warrington 1646, speculative Freemasonry must have existed before that date, perhaps not as fixed Lodges but as occasional ones to admit persons who were considered suitable to be made Masons. Just how long before has still to be discovered. We do know that there was also a Lodge, possibly of a speculative nature, in nearby Chester around the same time.

So which theory do we go by; could it have a bit of both? The desire to bring about social change, the need to support one another in hard times and the opportunity which was available in the guild Lodges to allow non-operative and highly intelligent gentlemen to join the ranks. Was it then that we became a speculative organisation?

Brethren, much as I would like to give you a definitive answer, I am afraid our origins remain a puzzle which has yet to be solved.

Which is the Oldest Lodge?

It is not easy to answer this question mainly due to lack of records. However, what we can say is that in the early days Lodges were not permanent like they are today, but were what is known as 'occasional' Lodges, where groups of Freemasons met to hold a Lodge to 'initiate' a candidate.

They did not meet in a Masonic Halls until the early 1800s, and even then there were many more who still met in hostelries up and down the country well into the latter part of that century. Wigan did not have its first Masonic Hall until 1874, when Leader Buildings in King Street were opened. If you are ever in the area, take a look from the opposite side of the road and you can see Masonic symbols as part of the ornamentation of the building, which is now a wine bar.

We have of course the diary of Elias Ashmole who claimed that he was made a Mason at Warrington at 4.30p.m. on 16 October 1646. In his diary he says:

'I was made a Free Mason at Warrington in Lancashire, with Col. Henry Mainwaring of Kerincham in Cheshire. The names of those that were then of the Lodge; Mr Rich Penket Warden, Mr James Collier, Mr Rich Sankey, Henry Littler, John Ellam and Hugh Brewer.'

The words 'Free Mason' in this extract constitute the first known use of the term carrying a speculative or symbolic meaning.

James Anderson, who wrote the first *Book of Constitutions* in 1723, claimed that Lodges had been established in London during the rebuilding after the Great Fire of London in 1666; however, he was unable to provide any evidence to substantiate his claim.

Randle Holme's Lodge in Chester may have met regularly from around 1665, as he writes in his *Academie of Armory*, he was a Deputy Garter King of Arms in 1688: '*I cannot but honour the Fellowship of the Masons because of its antiquity, and the more as being (myself) a member of that Society called Freemasons.*'

The present Time Immemorial Lodge of Antiquity No. 2 of London is believed to be the 'The Old Lodge at St. Pauls' referred to by Anderson as meeting in 1693. There is no evidence to confirm this, although there is a copy of the Old Charges dated 1683 which has always been in the possession of the Lodge.

In the old Lodge at York there is a minute book (which the author has seen himself) dated 1712 showing that it met regularly to make Masons, and V. W. Bro. Neville Barker Cryer has shown that Lodges met in that city to make Masons in the early 1600s. However, these were connected with operative Lodges.

It is not until 1726 that we have minutes of a Lodge which was purely speculative. These belonged to a Lodge which met at The Rummer & Grapes Tavern, Finch Lane, London on 2 February 1726. Even for the first Grand Lodge, formed in 1717 in London, there are no minutes for the first six years of its existence.

So to answer the question: Which is the oldest Lodge? I am sorry to disappoint you, we simply do not know.

Why the Square and Compasses?

The Basic Principles for Grand Lodge Recognition in the *Book of Constitutions* of the United Grand Lodge of England states at No. 6 that: '*the three Great Lights of Freemasonry (namely, the Volume of the Sacred Law, the Square and the Compasses) shall always be exhibited when the Grand Lodge or its subordinate Lodges are at work, the chief being the Volume of the Sacred Law.*'

Why did we choose the Square and Compasses as the outward signs of Freemasonry? Well, they probably stem from our medieval ancestors - and it may not have been uncommon in the Middle Ages and later to have a hostelry which displayed as its sign the Square and the Compasses to indicate that stonemasons and other craftsmen were likely to meet there. And since many craftsmen travelled from place to place to find work in those days, they might find suitable employment by visiting such an establishment.

Incidentally, the sign of the Square and Compasses was also used by other

Square and Compasses –
English Craft.

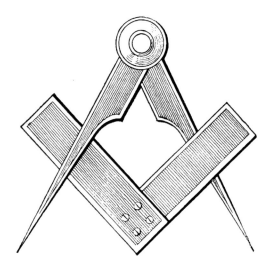

craftsmen - such as carpenters - but mainly by the stonemasons. In ancient Rome there is a square and compass design in the stonework on the outside of the Pantheon, designed by Hadrian in AD 125.

But how many of us know that the Square and the Compasses signified two different classes of craftsman, for which a long seven year apprenticeship had to be served before you became elected a 'fellow of the craft'? The square in stonemasons' terms relates to 'straight' or 'square' masons, the makers of stone with straight edges which sit one on top of the other with remarkable precision, as can be seen in many of our splendid cathedrals and other notable buildings. The compasses, on the other hand, denote the 'round' or 'arch' mason - a different and some would say a superior skill used to produce the beautiful arched naves of churches and doorways at the entrance to many of our buildings.

The Society of Free Masons, Rough Masons, Wallers, Slaters, Paviors, Plaisterers and Bricklayers of Durham was given a new charter by Bishop Morton in 1638. On its coat of arms, issued later, we see two supporters on either side of a shield, the one on the left-hand side, a craftsman, has a square in his hand and is wearing jacket which is blue, whilst the craftsman on the right is holding the compasses and his jacket is red.

Now perhaps you can see why we have the blue of the Craft and the red of the Royal Arch; however, those colours are of course also significant in the Mark Degree, reflecting its connection via the 'Keystone', which is a result of the combination of the two skills, with the Craft and the Royal Arch.

Under the English Constitution, only the Square and Compasses are shown as an emblem. However, in Scotland and America a letter 'G' is shown in the centre of the Square and Compasses. It is incorrect to show a 'G' in the Sq & C in English Freemasonry.

Would You Like to Write a Short Talk?

Frequently, Brethren have the desire to write a talk but don't really know how to start. The following is designed to help them along their way.

To write a talk may take some time, but there is no 'magic' solution involved and you may have to make several attempts before you are satisfied with your work.

The first thing to do is to decide on a subject. This could be something as simple as, for example: Why do we use the Square and Compasses as the commonly recognised symbol of Freemasonry?

There are many excellent books which you could read, which may give you an idea of a subject e.g. Harry Carr's *Freemason at Work* or Bernard Jones' *Freemasons Guide and Compendium.*

The Rev. Neville Barker Cryer has written several books which could help you, including: *I Just Didn't Know That* or *Did You Know This Too?* Often, these will be available via your local Masonic library or via a Brother who you happen to know is well informed on the history or symbolism of Freemasonry. They will often be more than delighted to help you with your research into your chosen subject. Many regalia manufacturers also sell Masonic books.

Do not be put off by the fact that someone may have written about something before, as your talk will be your personal interpretation of the chosen subject. On the other hand, you can try and write about a theme which your intended audience does not know anything about.

Once you have chosen your subject, read up on it and make notes as you go along of any aspects you find interesting or informative.

Do not be frightened by that word 'research'; it is not as difficult as many people think! It is, after all, a similar word to 'search' - and that is all that you are doing when you are gathering your material; you are just 'looking' for something.

There are two kinds of 'research': *primary research,* that is looking at original sources, e.g. the minutes of an old Lodge in your town which has not been written about before, or *secondary research,* using material which other people have written and published about a subject.

Once you have your basic material, try and put it into some sort of order for the talk you intend to give. Make a plan of your talk. Where do you want to start? What do you actually want to get across to your audience? What are the essential features of your subject matter?

Remember that every story has a beginning, a middle and an end. And always remember the maxim: '*Failing to plan is planning to fail.*'

Sort your notes, put them in the order in which you want to put your subject across and write out your talk. Keep your sentences fairly short and easy to follow. Don't forget to add your facts and give the Brethren something to think about.

You may have to try several times before find the one that works and flows the best. Do not be afraid to ask someone to read your draft talk; often a critical appraisal will help you!

The topics for a Masonic talk are almost endless. However, here is a list of some which may interest you, and others:

Masonic ritual
Masonic artefacts
Masonic music
Masonic stories
Masonic personalities
Local Lodge histories
Anti-Masonry
Women and Freemasonry
Differences in constitutions
Relationships with various churches
Masonic poems
Masonic postage stamps
and many other subjects of interest to Masons.

And, finally, remember that if you use established sources, please do not be afraid to make a reference to them, either in the body of your paper or at the end in the form of a reference list. After all, it shows you have 'researched' your subject thoroughly. If you have used other people's material you should always acknowledge it – it is only common courtesy and you wouldn't want to be accused of plagiarism, would you?

CHAPTER 2

Anti-Masonry Part 1

Anti-Masonry is far from a new phenomenon - it has been going on almost since Freemasonry began.

The first published attack on Freemasonry was in a leaflet distributed in London in 1698, accusing Masons as being '...*this devilish set of men...*', based on religious grounds.

On 7 July 1722, a letter was published in a London newspaper, accusing Masons of being a pretentious and illegal association referring to them as: '...*a set of low gentry amongst our artificers, who lately make a great bluster amongst us.*'

The following year, 1723, saw the publication of a bawdy poem *The Free Masons*, which suggested that Masons were notoriously heavy drinkers and sexual libertines, with a sordid reputation as far as women were concerned. It even ran to a second and third edition. The full poem can be read in Wallace McLeod's book *The Grand Design*. When it was published again in 1944 by those well-known Masonic scholars Knoop, Jones and Hamer, they printed only 158 out of the 366 lines, stating that: '*We have omitted portions displeasing to modern tastes.*'

In 1738, the Pope issued a Bull or Decree and forbade all Catholics to join Freemasonry accusing it of '*perverting the hearts of the simple*' and working against the Catholic Church.

Some years later, the 'Morgan Affair' arose in the USA, when Masons were accused of murdering William Morgan who had threatened to publish all their rituals after he had been refused permission to enter a Lodge in New York. He disappeared, and although some unscrupulous politicians and the media made the most of the story, it was pure speculation.

This affair created much anti-Masonic feeling and led to the formation of an Anti-Masonic Party, which even nominated a Presidential candidate.

The upshot was that Morgan was never found and nobody was charged with his murder. He simply disappeared. However, the damage had been done - which resulted in the number of Lodges falling from 480 to 82 in a three-year period. Many Lodges closed, particularly those on the East Coast, never to open again, and it took Freemasonry many years to recover from the scandal.

One of the worst periods of anti-Masonry in the 1800s was when a French pornographer, Léo Taxil, decide to turn against Masonry when his true character was discovered after he had been initiated into a Lodge in Paris and subsequently expelled.

Taxil published several anti-Masonic books and was the darling of the Catholic Church until he revealed at a public meeting in Paris in April 1897 that it had all been a hoax and he had conned the Church into supporting him. The audience received these revelations with indignation and contempt and he was forced to escape from the meeting with help of the police. However, he was less concerned, as he had made a fortune and he retired to Sceaux in the southern region of Paris, where he died at the age of 57.

Throughout the 20th century, Freemasonry was attacked many times. In the second part of this paper we will look at some of those attacks which have been carried out by Hitler and the Nazi regime and later by the Church of England and the Methodist Church.

Anti-Masonry - Part 2

During the 20th century, Freemasonry came under attack in several countries, not least in Germany prior to and during World War 2. In 1908, the Craft was revived in Russia after being closed down by Tsar Alexander I in 1822; however, it did not last long and it went out of existence again in 1922 under the Bolsheviks.

Under the Nazi regime, Freemasonry was banned and its members hunted down. They were beaten, imprisoned and sometimes killed. Masonic temples were sacked and destroyed - the temple in Jersey being a prime example. Propaganda against Freemasons and its alleged connection with Judaism was rife.

In 1925, Mussolini passed an anti-Masonic law in Italy and Masonry was suppressed in Portugal in 1931 and in Spain by Franco in 1941. Romania followed in 1948 and Hungary in 1950. Soekarno banned it in Indonesia in the 1960s and it was banned in Pakistan in 1972. The Ayatollah Khomeini took action against Freemasonry in Iran in 1979. And so it goes on. What is clear is that the type of regime which prohibits Freemasonry is usually a dictatorship of some type. Freemasonry has since recovered in some of the countries mentioned above, but by no means all of them.

In the 1990s, Freemasonry in the USA suffered from scurrilous attacks by a faction within the Southern Baptist Church. They tried time and time again to have church members barred from membership of the Craft. They failed - but their endeavours crossed the Atlantic when much of their anti-Masonic literature was published in the UK and taken up by different churches. Interestingly, whilst writing my paper on anti-Masonry, I was able to buy several anti-Masonic books from the Christian Bookshop located under the Masonic

Hall in Wigan which was owned and rented out by the Masons!

The Presbyterian Church of Ireland voted at the General Assembly in 1992 to 'disapprove of involvement in Freemasonry' on the part of its members. The same church in Scotland had done the same thing earlier in 1979. The Methodist Church in England made a similar attempt in 1986 and in the same year the Church of England also 'had a go' – although somewhat inconclusively.

The former Local Government Management Board issued advice to local authorities, requiring applicants to declare if they were a Freemason or not. This was clear discrimination and it took several years to remove.

Chris Mullin MP famously tried to introduce a Register of Freemasons in the Police and Judiciary in 1998. The attempt failed. He eventually admitted that he had only read *one* book on Freemasonry, the infamous *Inside the Brotherhood*, a book which frankly was so untrue as to be almost a joke.

Grand Lodge changed its policy towards anti-Masonry some years ago from remaining silent on attacks, so that now whenever somebody 'has a go' we respond vigorously. This has paid off and the image of Freemasonry is improving for the better day by day.

Finally, I will leave you with this thought: the surest guarantee of our freedom from criticism is the integrity of individual Freemasons themselves.

The Grand Lodge in Wigan

The Union of the two rival Grand Lodges, the Moderns and the Antients which had existed in England previously, took place in 1813 and these became the United Grand Lodge of England. For a few years all went reasonably well, until dissent broke out in Liverpool when in 1818 Lodge No. 31, trying to establish itself as the senior Lodge in the city, wrote to the Board of General Purposes seeking to have a Lodge whose membership had fallen below seven not to be considered a regular Lodge, and that the Warrant should be declared void and the number put at the disposal of Grand Lodge.

The Board did not reply and so members of the Liverpool Lodge decided to write directly to the Grand Master, the Duke of Sussex, complaining in quite strong terms about the lack of response from the Board of General Purposes. Again they did not receive a reply.

The letter was not well received in London, and Grand Lodge accused No. 31 of a Breach of Masonic Law and summoned them to appear to explain themselves. They refused.

The Liverpool Lodge remained obdurate and several Wigan Masons from the Lodge of Sincerity No. 486 and the Lodge of Integrity No. 74 joined the

Grand Lodge certificate from the re-formed Antients Grand Lodge also known as the Grand Lodge in Wigan 1847.

dissenters. The dispute rumbled on for another two years with even more Lodges joining in. Finally, Grand Lodge's patience was becoming exhausted and they again demanded that Liverpool No. 31 appear at Grand Lodge to explain themselves. Again they refused. Several Brethren then retracted their support for No. 31 after expulsion was threatened and they sought a pardon from Grand Lodge; however, thirty-four Brethren refused to comply and finally No. 31 was struck off and the Brethren were expelled from Freemasonry for ever. Another Liverpool Lodge, Sea Captains No. 120, complained, stating that they would leave United Grand Lodge if No. 31 was not reinstated. They were also expelled from Freemasonry for ever.

Undeterred, the dissenters re-formed the Grand Lodge of Free and Accepted Masons According to the Old Institutions (or Constitutions), the former Antients Grand Lodge, initially in Liverpool. It met a few times in the city; however, a dispute arose between the Wigan Masons and their Liverpool colleagues when the Grand Secretary embezzled the entire Grand Lodge funds. This was further exacerbated when the new Grand Secretary complained that the Wigan Masons had not paid their subscriptions.

Consequently, the Grand Lodge only met a couple of times after that and by 1838 the Wigan Masons had decided to take it over. It operated out of the town and became known as the Grand Lodge in Wigan. It had a maximum of eleven Lodges on its roll but eventually it became reduced to one, the Lodge of Sincerity No.1. It had its final meeting as a Grand Lodge in 1860.

However, Sincerity continued stubbornly on its own for 90 years until 1913 when it came back under United Grand Lodge as Sincerity Lodge No. 3677, and to this day it still meets at Bryn Masonic Hall, Wigan.

The above has been the subject of much Masonic debate and several books have been written about it - and an utterly fascinating story it is. However, Gould, in his mammoth *History of Freemasonry,* only gave it a one-page mention.

He Was Master of His Lodge Twelve Times

What was that? Master of his Lodge *twelve* times; surely it can't be true! However, it *is* true, Brethren, and before I tell you who it was, I must first give you the background to the story.

The Lodge of Antiquity No. 178, (originally 235) holds a Warrant dated 26 May 1786, and it may be considered a daughter Lodge of the Lodge of Antiquity No. 146 of Bolton, Lancashire. At a meeting of the latter Lodge, Richard Holmes of Wigan, innkeeper, was initiated. He was later passed and raised at an emergency meeting at his home, the Queen's Head, Market Place, Wigan. On Wednesday 21 June 1786, a Grand Lodge under the Antients was held by dispensation at the Queen's Head and the Lodge of Antiquity No 235 was consecrated.

Initially, the Lodge appears to have developed quite well - that is until around the middle of the 19th century when it began to go through a depressed period. In 1844, a Brother Henry Miller's name appears in the minutes, when he was appointed to represent the Lodge at the celebration of the laying of the foundation stone of Literary & Philosophical Hall, Preston, Lancashire. Prior to this, he appears in the members list from 1815 and is shown as Junior Warden on 22 December 1817 and on 18 May 1818. He appears as Senior Warden on 18 January 1819. On 27 December of that year, he is shown as Worshipful Master for the first time. During this period it was not uncommon for a WM to serve for six months; therefore there would be two Installations per year usually around St. John the Baptist Day, 24 June, and again at St. John the Evangelist Day on 27 December. Hence, the 'Festivals of St. John'.

He does not appear again until 18 July 1838, when he is installed as Master, and again on 28 January 1839. Then we have a sequence of Installations of Brother Henry Miller as follows: 13 Jan 1840, 4 January 1841 and 27 December 1841. Then there is a gap until 17 February 1845 and again in 1846 (no date) followed by a further gap until 8 January 1849, when he appears as Senior Warden and the same in January 1850. On 15 March 1851 he is shown as Master once more, followed by a further period in the Chair in January 1852 and again on 21 February 1853.

He was installed for the last time in the Chair on 21 January 1856. This is a total of twelve times over a period of thirteen years and whilst this may not be a record, it is significant when you consider that in addition he also served as Warden of the Lodge five times.

It is recorded that he and his close friend Thomas Holmes, who was Master in 1843 and 1844, would walk from Hindley, a distance of between three and four miles into Wigan, only to find that there was an insufficient number of Brethren to open their Lodge. However, Brother Holmes nevertheless always recorded the event and signed the record as Secretary. Eventually the Lodge recovered.

Brother Holmes died in 1858; however, it was another eleven years before Brother Miller passed to the Grand Lodge Above when he was buried alongside his old and beloved Brother in Hindley churchyard.

I am sure you will agree, it is indeed a remarkable story by any standards.

The City of Chester and its Masonic Significance

The significance of Chester in Masonic History is often overlooked, and very few know that a Masonic Lodge existed in the city in the mid-1600s. It is important when, as we know, through Elias Ashmole, there was a Masonic Lodge in nearby Warrington in 1646.

The name Randle Holme can be considered fairly common in Chester's history when you consider that no fewer than five persons of importance have borne that name. All were genealogists and heraldic painters. Randle Holme III (1627-1699) was the grandson of a deputy to a Garter King of Arms.

He wrote *Academie of Armory* in which he makes several references to Freemasonry. This may indicate a non-operative nature in the Fraternity during the seventeenth century. An account of his states:

'*A Fraternity or Society, or Brotherhood, or Company; are such in a corporation, that are of one and the same trade or occupation, who being joined together by oath and covenant, do follow such orders and rules, as are made, to be made for the good order, rule and support of such and every one of their occupations. These several fraternities are generally governed by one or two Masters and two Wardens, but most companies with us, by two Aldermen and two Stewards, the later, being to pay and receive what concerns them.*'

And in another passage he says:

'*I cannot but Honour the Fellowship of the Masons because of its Antiquity; and the more, as being a Member of that Society, called Free-Masons. In being conversant amongst them I have observed the use of these several tools following some whereof I have seen being borne in Coats of Armour.*'

He had previously referred to several tools without making any comment about them.

Holme, it would seem, had transcribed a copy of the *Harleian MS* and this and a scrap of paper with it were found in his effects, and written on it is the following:

'*There is several words and signs of a Freemason to be revealed to you which as you will answer; before God at the Great and terrible day of judgement you keep secret and not reveal the same to any in the hearing of any person but to the Masters and fellows of the said Society of Freemasons, so help me God etc.*'

There was also another note which probably referred to a Lodge already in existence; this listed the names of several members and most have been identified. Some were members of various trades, some masons and other building trades. There were also figures recorded on the note which may have referred to entrance fees and subscriptions.

A final and significant point is the fact that Cheshire was the first in the English Constitution to have a Provincial Grand Lodge when Col. Francis Columbine was elected first Grand Master at Chester in 1725.

Other Fraternal Societies

After Freemasonry emerged in the late 1600s and into the 18th century in England and Wales, other friendly societies and fraternal orders started to appear. It has been suggested that they used Freemasonry as the basis for their structure and that they copied some of its ideas such as ritual and regalia, and there is some evidence to support this theory.

What was their purpose? Well they did not have the same purpose as Freemasonry; they served their local communities by providing support and opportunities for families to save for their future by paying subscriptions into a fund from which in due course they were able to claim for sickness and perhaps a decent burial. What we must be aware of is the fact that there was no National Health Service and when sickness occurred, treatment had to be paid for.

Often they were a support network for local people where friendship groups were very important, so they were highly social bodies. But many had two sides to their activities: the financial, the 'friendly society' and the fraternal. 'Fraternal' according to *Chambers Dictionary* means: *'belonging to a brother or brethren; brotherly'*; Fraternity – *'the state of being brothers; a society formed on the principles of brotherhood.'*

So who were they? Well, several claim to be the oldest, and the following are not necessarily listed in their order of age.

One of the commonest is the Royal Antediluvian Order of Buffaloes. It is one the largest of the fraternal organisations and has branches throughout the United Kingdom. It is believed it was formed in London by stage artists and its motto is 'Unity, Liberty and Charity' and the principles of the Order are tolerance, brotherly love and good fellowship. It has similar regalia to Freemasons and has its own degrees and ritual. The discussion of politics or religion at its meetings is forbidden.

Another large and popular friendly and fraternal society is The Oddfellows. Formed in 1810, it had a widespread following in the UK, the USA and Australia. Unfortunately there were several breakaway movements and the USA was one of them, where they are now known as the Odd Fellows. One of the most prominent ones in the UK is the Independent Order of Odd Fellows

Royal Antediluvian Order of Buffaloes – Roll of Honour apron.

Royal Antediluvian Order of Buffaloes – commemorative jewels.

Oddfellows' chain jewels.

Manchester Unity Friendly Society. Its headquarters are in Manchester and it has Lodges spread across the UK. It too uses regalia and ritual and is based upon Christian principles. Its motto is 'Friendship, Love and Truth'. This Order is open to men and women.

The Druids are fairly well known, but many people think they only existed in the past; in fact they are thriving. The Ancient Order of Druids is the parent and founding order of the modern Druidic Societies, and was revived in the year 1781. Its object is to preserve and practise the main principles attributed to the early Druids, particularly those of justice, benevolence and friendship. As with other fraternal societies, the discussion of politics or religion is forbidden at its meetings. The Order is open to men only.

My final example is the Free Gardeners which was known to exist in Scotland in the early 1700s and it seems that they emulated the Freemasons in their structure. It is possible that the early Free Gardeners Lodges were a trade organisation for the many gardeners of the stately homes particularly in southern Scotland. The society had a moral dimension to its activities and many non-gardeners joined its ranks. Later it declined severely but was revived in Scotland around the year 2002. They wear aprons and the emblem of the Order is the Square and Compasses with a pruning knife across the centre.

Finally, there were over a thousand fraternal and friendly societies in the UK in the 19th century, most of which have now been confined to the history books.

Emblem of the Free Gardeners – the Square and Compasses with a pruning knife.

Jewel of the Free Gardeners.

The Two Grand Lodges

During the course of some of my talks you will hear me mention the Union of the two Grand Lodges of England in the early 19th century so I think it is a good idea to tell you a little about them.

The first Grand Lodge of England came about in 1717, as a result of four old Lodges all meeting in London who decided to form a Grand Lodge from the members of those four Lodges. The establishment of this first Grand Lodge took place on St. John the Baptist's Day, 24 June 1717, at the Goose and Gridiron alehouse near St. Paul's Cathedral which was designed by Sir Christopher Wren after the Great Fire of London in 1666. Its first Grand Master, of whom little is known, was Anthony Sayer, a Gentleman.

This Grand Lodge is regarded as the 'premier' Grand Lodge of England, as there was another one formed about 34 years later - The Grand Lodge of England According to the Old Institutions - in 1751, but its first Grand Master, Robert Turner, was not elected until two years later. Later the 3rd and 4th Dukes of Atholl served as Grand Masters; hence the name 'The Atholl Grand Lodge' as it commonly became known.

Some of the founders of this Grand Lodge are believed to have been Masons in London who had been initiated in Ireland and the ritual of this Grand Lodge varied very little from that worked in Irish or Scottish Lodges. They also became known as the 'Antients' because they claimed that they worked an older form of ritual than the original Grand Lodge, whom they nicknamed 'The Moderns' because the latter had varied the modes of recognition partly to counter 'exposures' and the illegal making of Masons in various hostelries, which was rife at that time.

So the older became the Moderns and the younger became the Antients or Atholl.

These two Grand Lodges were rivals until 1813 when they merged to become our present-day United Grand Lodge of England.

Wigan had one Lodge from each of the two Constitutions, both consecrated in the same year, 1786, and both are still in existence. The first one was the Lodge of Antiquity No.178 of June 1786 under the Antients and the other was the Lodge of Sincerity No. 304 in December 1786 under the Moderns Grand Lodge, now Sincerity Lodge No. 3677. Both co-existed in the town until 1823; however, after the Union the Lodge of Sincerity, along with several Lodges in the North-West broke away to re-form the Antients Grand Lodge. I will not say much more about that here as it is the subject of another paper.

The Union took several years to achieve: negotiations went on from 1805 until 1813 when eventually a compromise was reached. What was one of the major effects of the merger? Actually, the ritual was changed considerably. The Antients always claimed that theirs was the older and it was certainly more comprehensive than that of the Moderns. Some say the changes were detrimental to the Craft, taking away a lot of the symbolism of the old workings. On the other hand, the Moderns did not have a ceremony of the Installation of a Master prior to the Union; they were simply elected. So something was lost and something was gained.

So now, Brethren, when you hear me mention the Union you will know what I am talking about.

The York Rite

The city of York does possess many of the Old Charges and other Masonic documents but none relate to early or medieval ritual. As far as can be ascertained there is nothing which would distinguish the working of the oldest York Lodges from any other in England.

The York Rite is not a rite of English Freemasonry but is of American origin. Let me say straight away that the York Rite has little to do with York and comes from a perceived tradition in America; it would be better called the American Rite.

If you were to be an Initiate in a Craft Lodge in the Unites States, you would, as in England, progress to become a Fellowcraft and eventually a Master Mason and that is as far you can go until you progress through the Chair of the Lodge and become a Past Master, making you eligible for acting office in the Grand Lodge of the State in which you reside.

As there are no Provincial Grand Lodges in the USA, Grand Rank in one of the State Grand Lodges is the only possibility for progression, as no Past Ranks are conferred except in very high positions in the Grand Lodge.

Many Masons remain in a Craft - or 'Blue Lodge' as they are known - and having no desire to enter the world beyond the Craft, which in the USA is quite extensive, and simply remain members of their own Lodge.

After the Craft, Masons general choose one of two routes of progression to 'other' degrees: the York Rite and/or the Ancient and Accepted Scottish Rite. Both organisations work several additional degrees, with a presence in all States. The latter is a huge organisation divided into two jurisdictions: The Southern Jurisdiction (the larger), and the Northern Jurisdiction.

When the Antients Grand Lodge was formed in England in 1751, it was known as the Most Antient and Honourable Fraternity of Free and Accepted Masons According to the Old Institutions, but under the secretaryship of Laurence Dermott the words 'granted by His Royal Highness Prince Edwin of York in 926 AD' were added, leading to the Antients sometimes being called 'Ancient York Masons'.

How the York Rite began is rather obscure. In his most recent book, *The Complete Idiot's Guide to Freemasonry* S. Brent Morris suggests that because the Antients Grand Lodge of England set up Lodges in the United States and used the term 'Ancient York Masons' in their title, those Lodges of Antients heritage called themselves 'Ancient York Masons' too.

But what is the York Rite? It is a system of degrees beyond the Craft that are mostly small, local, sometimes rural bodies spread right across the USA, which has as its parents, three main bodies: the Royal Arch, the Royal & Select Masters (or Cryptic degrees) and the Knights Templar and many, many more, too numerous to mention in this short paper.

Finally, there is a branch of the York Rite in this country, but we are not permitted to associate with it.

Women and Freemasonry

Many people misunderstand Freemasonry and think it is an organisation solely for men. However, they would be wrong.

Freemasonry under the United Grand Lodge England forbids women to be members of its Fraternity, but how many know that there are at least four Grand Lodges in England which admit women as members. Two are for women only and the other two for men and women.

Just as women are not allowed to attend our meetings, men are not allowed to attend theirs. However, that leaves the 'men and women' organisations. Well, men are not allowed to attend their meetings either and if they did they would probably be the subject of Masonic discipline. However, socially they do mix quite a lot and vice versa, and I have attended several events organised by friends who are lady Masons. Of course they are involved in raising money for various charities in the same way as male Masons.

There are two separate women's Grand Lodges:

The Order of Women Freemasons – The Honourable Fraternity of Antient Freemasonry - whose address is in Pembroke Gardens, London. They were founded in 1908. Their ritual is virtually identical to ours.

The other Order is: The Honourable Fraternity of Freemasons – a Women's Masonic fraternity. It is based in Finchley Road, London, and it was founded from the other women's group as a breakaway movement. Their ritual is also almost identical to ours.

The third Order is: The International Order of Co-Freemasonry Le Droit Humain - British Federation. They are based in Surbiton, Surrey, and are connected, as the title suggests, to many similar organisations around the world. The British branch of Le Droit Humane was founded in England in 1902. They work a ritual according to the Ancient and Accepted Scottish Rite and are therefore not compatible with the other three Orders.

The fourth Order is: The Grand Lodge for Men and Women which is based in Russell Square in London. This Order was only founded in 2001 and has Lodges mainly based in the South of England. As before, they rely on the same basic principles of recognition as United Grand Lodge and work a similar ritual to ours.

The Grand Lodge for Men and Women is a breakaway movement from Co-Masonry.

Certainly the women-only Orders are on good terms with United Grand Lodge and they sometimes meet to discuss matters of mutual interest. However, I have no information in this respect regarding the men and women's organisations.

CHAPTER 3

Did I?

Did I help or hurt today Lord?
Is anyone happier that I passed this way?
Will anyone remember that I spoke to them today?
And when the day is over and toiling time is through
Will someone say a kindly word, for me, for you?
I wonder can I say in parting, from a day that's slipping fast
Did I help a single brother? From the many that I passed?
Is a single heart rejoicing? Over what I did or said?
Does someone, whose hopes were fading, ?now with
new hope look ahead
Did I win this day or lose it? Was it well or poorly spent?
Did I leave a trail of kindness or a scar of discontent?
As I close my eyes in slumber, to the Architect above I pray
That I've earned one more tomorrow, by the good I did today.

Do You Remember Me?

This is a letter written by a Brother to his Lodge:

It amuses me now to hear that Freemasonry spends so much time looking for new members when I was there all the time.

Do you remember me?

I am the Brother that came to every meeting, but nobody paid any attention to me. I tried several times to be friendly, but everyone seemed to have his own friends to talk to and to sit with. I sat with them several times, but they didn't pay much attention to me.

I hoped somebody would ask me to join one of the committees or to somehow participate and contribute, but no one did.

Do you remember me?

Finally, because of an illness I missed a meeting. At the next meeting no one asked me where I had been. I suppose it didn't matter much whether I was there or not. On the next meeting date, I decided to stay at home and watch a good TV programme.

When I attended the next meeting, no one asked me where I had been the meeting before. You might say that I'm a good sort of a chap, a good family man, I hold a responsible job and I love and help my community.

Do you know who else I am? I am the member who never came back.

Do you remember me?

The Old Master's Wages

I met a dear old man today
Who wore a Masonic pin.
It was old and faded like the man,
Its edges were worn quite thin.

I approached the park bench where he sat,
To give the old brother his due.
I said, 'I see you've travelled east,'
He said, 'I have, have you?'

I said, 'I have, and in my day
Before the all seeing sun,
I played in the rubble, with Jubala
Jubalo and Jubalum.'

He shouted, 'Don't laugh at the work my son,
It's good and sweet and true,
And if you've travelled as you said,
You should give these things their due.'

The word, the sign, the token,
The sweet Masonic prayer,
The vow that all have taken,
Who've climbed the inner stair.

The wages of a Mason,
Are never paid in gold,
But the gain comes from contentment,
When you're weak and growing old.

You see, I've carried my obligations,
For almost fifty years.
It has helped me through the hardships
And the failures full of tears.

Now I'm losing my mind and body,
Death is near but I don't despair,
I've lived my life upon the level,
And I'm dying upon the square.
Sometimes the greatest lessons
Are those that are learned anew,
And the old man in the park today
Has changed my point of view.

To all Masonic brothers,
The only secret is to care.
May you live your life upon the level,
May you part upon the square.

The Summer of a Man's Life

J. David Jacobs PM
Miami Lodge No. 16, Cincinnati, Ohio

Every Mason is familiar with that excerpt from Ecclesiastes 12: *'Remember now thy Creator in the days of thy youth.'* Yet few of us have ever tried to understand this fine poem of life and death. The ancient Rabbis of the Talmud interpreted this poem and you will have a greater appreciation of its beauty when you have read it.

The poem begins with fine admonition by King Solomon: *'remember now thy Creator in the days of thy youth, while evil days come not, nor the years draw nigh, when thou shalt say, I have no pleasure in them'.* This refers, of course, to the advent of old age.

'While the sun, or the light, or the moon, or the stars be not darkened'. This means in old age there is a general decay of the powers and faculties of the mind. The understanding is obscured, the memory fails and the will becomes feeble and cold.

'Nor the clouds return after the rain'. This refers to the succession of

125

infirmities and pains which attend the winter of a man's life. *'In the day when the keepers of the house shall tremble'* refers to the arms and hands which tremble in old age. *'And the strong men shall bow themselves'.* This alludes to the lower limbs which bend forward and weaken in advancing age. It may also refer to the spine which tends to bend as the years take their toll. *'And the grinders cease because they are few'.* Here the author speaks of the loss of teeth so common among the aged.

'And those that look out of the windows be darkened'. Here the windows connote the eyes which no longer function properly and vision becomes dim.

'And the doors shall be shut in the streets when the sound of grinding is low'. This describes the common facial expression seen in the elderly when the lips are compressed and flattened because of the lack of teeth. Since gums are used for mastication, the diet changes to soft food and the sound of trituration is gone. *'And he shall rise up at the sound of the bird'.* Man sleeps so lightly in old age that he is aroused from his sleep by the twittering of a small bird. *'And all the daughters of music shall be brought low'.* Music no longer charms the old man as his hearing has become impaired.

'Also, when they shall be afraid of that which is high, and fears shall be in the way'. Here we find the poetic reference to the difficulty to the old man of climbing hills or ascending stairs. *'And the almond tree shall flourish'.* The almond flower is white and refers to the grey hair of the aged. *'And the grasshopper shall be a burden'.* In the weakness of old age weights cannot be borne and even light labour becomes burdensome. *'Or ever the silver be loosed'.* The silver cord is supposed to denote the spinal cord which passes through the entire length of the spine and is weakened by old age. *'Or the pitcher be broken at the fountain, or the wheel broken at the cistern'.* The fountain can only describe the heart, which, weakened in old age, can no longer pump blood around the circulatory system.

Here we have a wonderful description of the dry, the emaciated, querulous old man. All the physical signs indicate the approach of the time *'man goeth to his long home, and the mourners go about the streets. Then shall the dust return to the earth as it was; and the spirit shall return to the God who gave it.'* In this last sentence King Solomon expresses his belief in the immortality of the soul, which all good Masons have never doubted.